ICFA Continuing Education
Derivatives in Portfolio Management

Proceedings of the AIMR seminar "Using Derivatives in Managing Portfolios"

November 13–14, 1997
Chicago, Illinois

Don M. Chance, CFA
Joanne M. Hill
Thomas S.Y. Ho
Maarten L. Nederlof

Frank K. Reilly, CFA, *moderator*
David C. Shimko
Brian D. Singer, CFA, *moderator*
John Zerolis

To obtain the *AIMR Publications Catalog,* contact:
AIMR, P.O. Box 3668, Charlottesville, Virginia 22903, U.S.A.
Phone 804-980-3668; Fax 804-980-9755; E-mail info@aimr.org
or
visit AIMR's World Wide Web site at **www.aimr.org**
to view the AIMR publications list.

ICFA Continuing Education is published monthly seven times a year in May, May, June, June, July, August, and September by the Association for Investment Management and Research, P.O. Box 3668, Charlottesville, Virginia 22903, U.S.A. This publication is designed to provide accurate and authoritative information with regard to the subject matter covered. It is sold with the understanding that the publisher is not engaged in rendering legal, accounting, or other professional services. If legal advice or other expert assistance is required, the services of a competent professional should be sought. Periodicals postage paid at the post office in Richmond, Virginia, and additional mailing offices.

Copies are mailed as a benefit of membership to CFA® charterholders. Subscriptions also are available at US$100 for one year. Address all circulation communications to ICFA Continuing Education, P.O. Box 3668, Charlottesville, Virginia 22903, U.S.A.; Phone 804-980-3668; Fax 804-980-9755. For change of address, send mailing label and new address six weeks in advance.

Postmaster: Send address changes to the Association for Investment Management and Research, P.O. Box 3668, Charlottesville, Virginia 22903.

ISBN 0-935015-22-1
Printed in the United States of America
June 1998

Editorial Staff
Terence E. Burns, CFA
Book Editor

Bette Collins
Editor

Jaynee M. Dudley
Production Manager

Roger Mitchell
Assistant Editor

Christine P. Martin
Production Coordinator

Lois A. Carrier
Diane B. Hamshar
Composition

Contents

Foreword

"Derivatives" is a bad word to many in the investment management industry. A few highly publicized disasters have given derivatives a bad rep. The use of derivative instruments is not without risk, of course, but the main point to remember is that these wonderfully flexible instruments are legitimate (and sometimes unique) aids to controlling portfolio risk and enhancing portfolio return. One of the intentions of the seminar from which this proceedings is drawn was to separate perception from reality—to clarify how and when derivatives add value and how and when the problems creep in.

The presentations in this proceedings concentrate on the tools for using derivatives successfully and the processes for reducing the risk of using them. The "how to" discussions range from the great variety of equity and fixed-income derivatives to using derivatives in international investing. The "what to avoid" discussions pinpoint past control problems in derivatives use, the valuation processes managers can use to accurately measure and evaluate the risks and returns specific derivatives will introduce, and the firmwide processes senior managers can institute to mitigate control problems.

We extend special thanks to the moderators of "Using Derivatives in Managing Portfolios"—Frank K. Reilly, CFA, College of Business Administration at the University of Notre Dame, and Brian D. Singer, CFA, Brinson Partners—for their help and skillful management of the seminar. We also wish to thank all the speakers: Don M. Chance, CFA, Virginia Tech; Joanne M. Hill, Goldman, Sachs & Company; Thomas S.Y. Ho, BARRA, Incorporated; Maarten Nederlof, Deutsche Morgan Grenfell Inc.; David C. Shimko, Bankers Trust Company, New York; and John Zerolis, Swiss Bank Corporation.

We are pleased to make this proceedings available to you. We believe it will be a useful addition to your library of continuing education materials.

Terence E. Burns, CFA
Vice President
Educational Products

Biographies

Don M. Chance, CFA, is First Union Professor of Financial Risk Management at Virginia Tech (Virginia Polytechnic Institute and State University) and conducts research and consulting in financial derivatives and risk management. He is the author of *An Introduction to Derivatives* and associate editor of the *Journal of Financial Engineering* and the *Journal of Derivatives*. Professor Chance serves as an advisor to the Chicago Board of Trade and the New York Stock Exchange. He holds a Ph.D. from Louisiana State University.

Joanne M. Hill is co-head of the global equity derivatives research group at Goldman, Sachs & Company. Prior to joining Goldman Sachs, she served on the finance faculty of the University of Massachusetts at Amherst. Ms. Hill serves as managing editor of *Derivatives Quarterly* and on the editorial boards of the *Financial Analysts Journal* and *Financial Management*. She is a member of the review board for the Research Foundation of the Institute of Chartered Financial Analysts, the board of the Futures Industry Institute, and the board of trustees of the Financial Management Association. Ms. Hill holds an undergraduate degree from American University, an M.A. in international affairs from George Washington University, and an M.B.A. and Ph.D. in finance and quantitative methods from Syracuse University.

Thomas S.Y. Ho is president and founder of Global Advanced Technology Corporation and a professor at the Stern School of Business at New York University. Previously, he was a research analyst at the government bond trading desk for Yamaichi Securities. Mr. Ho is the author of the book *Strategic Fixed Income Investment* and numerous articles published in leading journals, and he is the editor of *Fixed Income Management: Issues and Solutions*, *Fixed Income Investment: Recent Research*, and *Frontiers in Fixed Income*. He holds a Ph.D. in mathematics from the University of Pennsylvania.

Maarten L. Nederlof is managing director of global equity derivatives at Deutsche Morgan Grenfell. Previously a senior vice president at Capital Market Risk Advisors, he also served as partner and managing director of research and portfolio management at TSA Capital Management and was a founding member of the equity portfolio analysis and derivative research group at Salomon Brothers Inc. Mr. Nederlof studied chemistry and computer applications in the physical sciences at the University of Pennsylvania and the decision sciences at The Wharton School.

Frank K. Reilly, CFA, is the Bernard J. Hank Professor of Business Administration at the College of Business Administration at the University of Notre Dame and previously served as dean of the College. Prior to joining Notre Dame, he held positions as a professor at the University of Illinois at Urbana–Champaign, the University of Wyoming, and the University of Kansas; as a stock and bond trader for Goldman, Sachs & Company; and as a senior security analyst for the Technology Fund. Professor Reilly is author of the books *Investments* and *Investment Analysis and Portfolio Management* and editor of *Readings and Issues in Investments, Ethics and the Investment Industry*, and *High Yield Bonds: Analysis and Risk Assessment*. He is a member of the AIMR Board of Governors and chair of the Institute of Chartered Financial Analysts Board of Trustees. Professor Reilly holds a B.B.A. from the University of Notre Dame, an M.B.A. from Northwestern University, and a Ph.D. from the University of Chicago.

David C. Shimko is vice president in the Risk Management Advisory Group at Bankers Trust. Previously, he held positions as vice president and head of risk-management research for J.P. Morgan Securities (where he also served as head of commodity derivatives research), assistant professor of finance at the University of Southern California, and a private consultant to financial institutions. Mr. Shimko is the author of *Finance in Continuous Time: A Primer* and articles on strategic issues and the practice of risk management that have been published in academic and trade journals. He has also produced financial software packages. Mr. Shimko holds a B.A. in economics and a Ph.D. in managerial economics and finance from Northwestern University.

Brian D. Singer, CFA, is a partner and senior analyst at Brinson Partners. His articles on global asset management and performance attribution have appeared in various investment publications. Mr. Singer is a member of the AIMR Candidate Curriculum Committee and a review board member of the Research Foundation of the Institute of Chartered

Financial Analysts. He holds a B.A. from Northwestern University and an M.B.A. from the University of Chicago.

John Zerolis is the director of risk control at Swiss Bank Corporation and a teacher in the financial mathematics program at the University of Chicago.

He has developed visualization, simulation, and symbolic programming techniques for studying, valuing, and hedging equity, index, and foreign exchange options. Previously, Mr. Zerolis designed real-time equity option-trading and risk-control systems and created the fat-tail option-pricing model for O'Connor and Associates.

Overview: Derivatives in Portfolio Management

The phenomenal growth of the derivatives markets since the 1970s has been one of the most significant developments in financial markets in the past 25 years. In 1997, the notional amount of swaps outstanding was in the tens of trillions of dollars, the worldwide average daily volume of stock index futures was about $59 billion, and the worldwide average daily volume of index options was about $45 billion. Obviously, derivative instruments have come a long way from the first stock index options in the early 1970s.

The flexibility of derivative instruments to achieve a desired exposure or accomplish an intended strategy has been the primary reason for the proliferation of derivative applications in portfolio management. The first stock index options helped portfolio managers and investors manage broad equity market exposure. Now, when properly applied, derivatives allow management of specific exposure to virtually any source of risk—inflation, interest rate, equity market, currency, commodity, or catastrophe. The more accurately portfolio managers define their exposure to unique risks, the more tailored and exotic derivative applications become. Having the right tool for the task at hand holds true in construction, medicine, and portfolio management. Derivatives can be a very effective tool for the portfolio manager; the key is to select the instrument that best fits the intended strategy or objective.

Despite the potential benefits of derivatives, many clients and portfolio managers are reluctant to use them. Indeed, some plan sponsors forbid the use of any type of derivative. This derivatives phobia is the result of highly publicized disclosures of losses experienced by Procter & Gamble, Barings, the Orange County Investment Pool, and others. The lesson to learn from these debacles, however, is not to broadly restrict the use of derivatives but to control the risks of derivative use by using risk-measurement tools to quantify the firm's overall level of exposure and by developing a firmwide risk-management framework that is appropriate for the organization's size and structure. Such a framework avoids unintended applications of derivatives—such as speculation—and unintentional side effects—severe losses, lawsuits, and possibly bankruptcy.

The seminar from which this proceedings was developed was intended to give participants an understanding of derivatives applications in portfolio management—a topic of growing importance in global financial markets. Various authors in the proceedings draw on their extensive industry experience to provide overviews of equity, fixed-income, and currency derivatives applications and an understanding of how to measure volatility and correlation in pricing derivatives. Presentations also demonstrate how to apply value-at-risk (VAR) measures to portfolios containing derivatives, draw on lessons learned from public disclosures of derivatives losses, and explain the functions of a sound risk-management framework.

Derivative Applications

Equity, fixed-income, and currency derivatives are effective tools for managing exposure and implementing a wide variety of portfolio strategies.

On the equity side, Joanne Hill reviews the evolution of derivatives, explains the major types of equity derivatives, discusses the conditions that affect derivatives activity, and describes various methods of implementing equity derivatives strategies. She notes that the use and sophistication of derivative instruments have grown tremendously since the 1970s. Although the evolution of the derivatives markets stalled after the 1987 stock market crash, it picked up again in the early 1990s with the development of international derivatives markets and the growth of fixed-income derivative products.

Hill reviews the basic characteristics of futures and options in terms of valuation, trading volume, and volatility and explains how to add value with each instrument. She advises portfolio managers to understand how volatility and market direction, macroeconomic events, the regulatory environment, and liquidity influence the level of derivatives activity. Finally, Hill discusses four major types of derivative applications—efficient/enhanced fund management, asset allocation, view-driven strategies, and risk management.

The use of fixed-income derivative products grew enormously in the early 1990s. Don Chance points out the difference between bond derivatives and interest rate derivatives and discusses a host of fixed-income derivatives that allow portfolio managers to achieve almost any fixed-income exposure. Chance cautions that choosing the derivative that best fits the manager's strategy involves assessing whether the exposure being hedged is broad based or specific. Differences between exchange-traded and OTC fixed-income derivatives in terms of standardization, credit risk, transparency, liquidity, and costs can also affect which type of derivative should be used. Although each derivatives market is different, they are integrated with the money and capital markets through the term structure of interest rates and the credit risk structure of interest rates. Whether a portfolio manager desires to hedge interest rate risk or modify a portfolio's duration, understanding the characteristics and variations of forward rate agreements, interest rate options, swaps, swaptions, and interest rate futures will help the portfolio manager select the appropriate derivative for the intended strategy. One of the newest class of products—credit derivatives—adds a new dimension to buying and selling risk. Chance expects that this evolving market will improve loan pricing in fixed-income markets but will require coordinated pricing of credit risk and derivatives and advances in modeling credit risk.

Currency derivatives—ranging from generic cross-currency swaps to differential swaps to basket swaptions—represent some of the more complex applications of derivatives in portfolio management. Thomas Ho discusses how investors can use currency derivatives to manage a global fixed-income portfolio and describes the motivation behind their use. Ho demonstrates how generic currency swaps allow investors to hedge payments in foreign currencies, but he encourages derivatives users to think of swaps in terms of managing total return rather than hedging. He explains that a currency swap, conceptually, is merely a short position in one bond and a long position in another. Ho encourages counterparties to analyze each source of risk, and he illustrates the effects of alternative interest rate risks and currency risk on the "price surface" of several swap structures. He explains how investors can achieve exposure to a basket of currencies with basket options and how differential swaps allow investors to speculate on interest rate differentials between currencies.

Individual derivative applications may accomplish certain objectives—such as international diversification—but investors should understand the effect derivatives have on total portfolio risk. Using VAR analysis and a "quality assurance" methodology, Ho demonstrates how each individual component of risk adds up to total risk for a portfolio or for the firm.

Measuring Derivatives Risk

Pricing, measuring volatility, and estimating the correlation between derivative instruments and asset classes often cause problems for portfolio managers and investors. John Zerolis cautions analysts that they need to understand the limitations of option-pricing models and the differences between alternative volatility measures. After pointing out that the human

mind can more quickly process visual images than words, Zerolis effectively uses pictures—triangles and tetrahedrons—to illustrate the mathematical relationships between volatility and correlation. Because the volatility and correlation of asset-class returns clearly depend on the currency in which returns are measured, Zerolis adds to his volatility-and-correlation geometry to illustrate the effect of currencies on volatility and correlation.

Highly publicized derivative losses highlight the importance of effectively quantifying derivative risk—a crucial step in *controlling* the risk. David Shimko explains how VAR, although it has its limitations, provides a comprehensive view of a portfolio's overall risk and can be used to quantify inherent market risk, determine the risks in view-driven strategies, and evaluate risks in terms of the potential returns. Shimko points out the challenges associated with measuring VAR, but because VAR clearly reveals component sources of risk, Shimko projects that it will be increasingly used to measure individual managers' performance and determine compensation.

Managing Derivatives Risk

An organization's best line of defense in controlling the risks of using derivatives is to develop sound risk-management policies. Although the complexity of some derivatives contributed to some of the recent derivatives debacles, the true culprits were a lack of oversight, inadequate checks and balances, and guidelines that did not take into account innovations in financial products. Maarten Nederlof discusses the key elements of a successful framework for risk management—adapting risk-measurement systems to innovations in financial markets and having written policies and procedures in place that fit the size and structure of the organization.

Pressure to create portfolio alpha prompts managers and traders to develop new products and invest in exotic securities and uncharted markets. Nederlof explains that these activities create a significant risk-management challenge for the firm. For example, traditional limitations on credit quality and duration become obsolete when derivative instruments have embedded credit options or create effective durations longer than stated maturities. Nederlof explains how risk-measurement and risk-management systems can help firms control risks as new products come onto the scene.

Documented policies governing the use of derivatives are an integral part of a successful risk-management framework. Nederlof considers the key elements in setting derivatives policies to include defining exactly what constitutes a derivative, establishing objectives for derivatives use, establishing limits on derivatives activity, making sure the back office can track and account for new derivative strategies and instruments, and making sure the firm has a minimum level of required expertise and resources. Counterparty selection and oversight, stress testing, adequate documentation, and reporting mechanisms reinforce the firm's risk-management infrastructure.

Conclusion

Derivatives offer portfolio managers and investors an incredible amount of flexibility to accomplish a wide variety of investment strategies. Derivatives can enhance returns and reduce risks, but if not used properly, they can also imperil the financial health of a firm and destroy value. In order to use these instruments effectively, users must understand what the instruments can accomplish, how they alter the risk–return profile of a portfolio, and how to operate a sound risk-management framework to prevent unintentional consequences. The authors of these presentations help readers understand the breadth of derivatives applications; cope with measuring the volatility, correlations, and currency effects in derivatives use; quantify derivatives risk; and manage the risks associated with these instruments.

Derivatives in Equity Portfolios

Joanne M. Hill
Co-Head of Global Equity Derivatives Research
Goldman, Sachs & Company

Equity derivatives can be effective in a wide range of strategies and have achieved broad acceptance by market participants. The market has evolved a great deal since the 1970s when stock options first began trading. Products range from simple replication of an index to such complex, sophisticated applications as creating synthetic international index exposure to equity-linked notes and swaps on volatility.

After 25 years of listed options trading, 15 years of listed futures trading, and the growth of the OTC markets, the importance and usefulness of equity derivatives in portfolio management has achieved broad recognition.[1] *Pension & Investment Age* surveys of the major pension funds indicate that about 50 percent of the largest 200 pension funds use derivatives in some way but only 10–11 percent of money managers admit to using them. The difference in percentage use is a function of the large number of money managers, the fact that most money managers are bottom-up stock pickers rather than macro investors, and the fact that many first-level derivatives applications are more top-down than bottom-up and, therefore, apply perhaps more to pension funds. Firms that were late to enter the derivatives market are beginning to hire derivatives experts and combine this expertise with the proper infrastructure—that is, risk-management systems and the middle- and back-office functions. This trend will ultimately give derivatives even broader recognition by market participants and will promote the successful use of these products.

This presentation is designed to provide a broad understanding of derivatives markets and then focus on derivatives applications for equity portfolios. It explains such important issues and concepts relating to derivatives as the evolution of equity derivatives, how products were developed to accomplish strategies, index replication, issues relating to futures and options, and conditions that affect the level of derivatives activity. The section on derivatives applica-

tions focuses on how derivatives can be used to enhance fund management, implement asset allocation and view-driven strategies, and manage risk. The main point is to encourage thinking of derivatives not as ends in themselves but as means to an end.

Evolution of Equity Derivatives

Strategies involving equity derivatives developed hand-in-hand with new equity products and implementation vehicles. In the early 1970s, the investing world focused on individual stock selection implemented through block trading of specific shares; selection of assets on the basis of portfolio concerns, efficient frontiers, and index funds were appreciated and studied more in the academic world than by practitioners.

Index funds are closely connected to the evolution and the development of derivatives. After the first index funds started in the mid-1970s, portfolio structuring based on quantitative principles became more important and stock options began trading. The 1970s were a great decade for the start-up and growth of covered-call writing because of the flat equity market returns—the average annual return on the S&P 500 Index from 1971 to 1980 was only approximately half a percent.

Strong equity market performance and the divergence of stock and bond returns in the 1980s changed the focus of derivatives. Derivatives strategies now centered on achieving exposure to U.S. equities, with applications involving tactical asset allocation and synthetic index funds. Portfolio insurance used futures to replicate a put option with the goal of protecting portfolio gains. Derivative strategies primarily involved stock index options and stock

---

[1]*Editor's note*: Some data in this presentation have been updated to reflect changes since the seminar date.

index futures. Although buying downside protection using index options and index futures attracted a lot of interest, one could do it only with dynamic hedging strategies because of the tight position limits on listed index options and low liquidity. The failure of portfolio insurance and its perceived connection to the stock market crash of 1987, plus the newness of the markets, led participants to reevaluate the use of derivatives. Although practitioners were interested in expanding their use of equity derivatives, the markets had not developed as fast as their interests, and they realized options were not going to work as planned. Dynamic hedging fell by the wayside, but synthetic investing with futures and basket, or portfolio, trading have both survived.

Proponents of derivatives adopted a bunker mentality for a few years; they spent most of their time trying to explain to regulators why derivatives were safe. In the 1990s, however, many new applications were developed. The main events were the development of international derivative markets and the growth in fixed-income OTC derivative markets. Competition from international exchanges and the growth in futures applications in the foreign markets spurred many U.S. institutions to take another look at derivatives.

The biggest growth in derivatives use in the 1990s has been in global asset allocation strategies. Another factor in the growth of equity derivatives was the development of long/short strategies, which use long index futures combined with a market-neutral position that is long a group of "in-favor" stocks and short stocks that are expected to underperform. OTC options and structured notes in equities fill in the gaps of listed derivatives trading and meet more customized needs. In contrast to fixed income, where the amount of OTC swaps and structured notes outstanding is greater than the amount of exchange-traded derivatives, the notional amount outstanding of OTC equity derivative products is a small fraction of the notional amount of listed equity derivatives.

Products Meet Strategies

Derivative products are used to make existing strategies more efficient or to make new strategies possible. Equity derivatives fit into two categories. The first group, stock or portfolio substitutes that have symmetrical returns, includes baskets, listed futures, and swaps. In this group, the derivatives bear the full risk and return of an underlying security or portfolio, but the underlying security's volatility does not affect the pricing. The second group, optionlike securities, encompasses listed options, OTC options, and market-indexed notes, which are fixed-income securities whose coupons and/or final payments depend on the return of a stock, portfolio of stocks, or market index. The volatility of the underlying security is a critical parameter in pricing these derivatives.

Index Replication

One of the basic concepts that underlie many derivatives applications is that they efficiently replicate exposure to an underlying index, such as the S&P 500, the Nikkei 225, or the Financial Times Stock Exchange (FTSE) 100. Basic derivative products, such as stock index futures and total-return swaps, easily and efficiently replicate the exposure to virtually any index or benchmark.

An investor has three ways of owning an index fund—buy the index, buy the future, or buy the swap. Buying the stocks in an index gives the investor the dividends, the ending value of the index (capital gains or losses), and any return on lending the stock. The alternative to buying the stocks is to buy a futures contract and invest in cash-equivalent portfolios— U.S. T-bills or money market securities. Buying a futures contract on the index gives the investor gains or losses on the future plus the interest income on investing the cash (net of initial margin) that would be otherwise used to buy stocks. The interest income on that portfolio serves in place of the dividend and offsets the loss as futures converge to the index level at expiration.

A swap operates in a similar way, but instead of the gains or losses occurring daily as the investor marks a listed futures position to market, the swap buyer pays interest in exchange for the total return of the index at the reset date, which is usually quarterly. The seller of the swap passes the return, or the move in the underlying portfolio, to the buyer and receives the interest payment. This return can be with or without dividends; the decision is up to the buyer and is reflected in the interest rate. Swap pricing is usually LIBOR plus or minus a spread, quoted in basis points, reflecting current market pricing and supply/demand conditions. As with futures, the buyer typically invests the cash in a money market portfolio; this portfolio generates the interest with which the buyer will pay the dealer for the return of the index via the swap. An investor will be indifferent between buying the underlying stocks and entering into a swap when interest income from the money market portfolio method equals the fixed- or floating-rate payment on the swap.

Futures Characteristics

Futures contracts produce symmetrical returns and bear the full risk and return of an underlying security or portfolio. The underlying security's volatility does not affect the pricing. Issues to consider in incorporating futures contracts in investment strategies include valuation, liquidity, tracking risk, and the cost advantage of using futures.

Valuation. The fair value of a futures contract equals the index value plus the expected interest income minus the dividend income. When determining fair value, the relevant time period is the days between settlement of a stock purchase on the day of the futures trade and the settlement of a stock sale at expiration. The key is the period over which the position needs to be financed by the arbitrageur. Fair value is derived from the difference between the dividends earned and the interest income over that time frame. The opportunity to arbitrage a mispriced future by buying stock and selling the future or vice versa is the basis for fair value.

The only uncertainty in the fair value is that investors must estimate dividend points to expiration, but this estimate can be made with a high degree of accuracy. **Table 1** provides some sample fair basis spreads and dividend yields for S&P 500 Index futures as of November 3, 1997. The interest rate driving futures arbitrage is best represented by the deposit rate in the global markets. Many people wonder why LIBOR is used instead of repurchase agreement (REPO) rates. In fixed-income investing, investors can borrow and lend Treasury securities in the REPO market. To conduct stock index arbitrage, investors must finance stock. So, in equities, the primary participants in index arbitrage are dealer firms that have high credit ratings, low-cost financing, and access to capital. Those firms usually use LIBOR or the U.S. Federal Reserve federal funds rate plus a credit spread. LIBOR yields are probably the closest thing to the financing rates that drive the arbitrage process.

For institutional clients, evaluation of calendar-spread pricing is critical because most people do not go in and out of a contract within an expiration cycle. Instead, they carry it over several cycles. Clients do at least as many calendar-spread trades as outright buying and selling of futures. So, investors need to consider the timing of shifting contracts from one expiration to another. For example, Table 1 provides

Table 1. S&P 500 Index Futures Valuation and Activity: November 3, 1997

A. Valuation

Index	Index/ Futures Close	Change	Fair Value	Actual Basis (spread)	Fair Basis (spread)	Percent Deviation versus Fair	Dividend Points	Dividend Yield	Simple Interest Yield	Settlement Days
S&P 500	914.62	10.94	—	—	—	—	—	—	—	—
12/19/97	924.00	20.90	919.22	9.38	4.60	0.52	2.34	1.96	5.69	48
03/20/98	933.50	21.15	928.71	18.88	14.09	0.52	6.20	1.79	5.75	139
06/19/98	943.30	21.10	938.41	28.68	23.79	0.53	10.12	1.76	5.80	230
09/18/98	952.70	21.35	948.45	38.08	33.83	0.47	14.04	1.75	5.87	321

B. Calendar Spread

Index	Actual Spread	Fair Spread	Quarterly Compound Yields			Simple Yields		
			Roll Yield	Forward Yield	Difference	Roll Yield	Forward Yield	Difference
S&P 500	—	—	—	—	—	—	—	—
12/19/97	—	—	—	—	—	—	—	—
03/20/98	9.50	9.49	5.99	5.94	0.05	5.78	5.73	0.05
06/19/98	19.30	19.19	6.03	5.96	0.07	5.86	5.79	0.07
09/18/98	28.70	29.23	5.95	5.98	–0.03	5.82	5.86	–0.03

C. Trading Activity

Index	Volume (number)	Volume ($ millions)	Open Interest
S&P 500	75,770	34,650	201,172
12/19/97	75,349	—	193,000
03/20/98	354	—	6,314
06/19/98	57	—	1,607
09/18/98	10	—	251

Note: U.S. dollar interest rates are derived from the Eurodollar futures curve; spot LIBOR rates are used for the period preceding the nearby Eurodollar contract. The "Trading Activity" data for the United States are shown on a one-day lag (two days ago).

a sample of the fair value calendar spreads for S&P 500 Index futures. An investor can determine the fair spread of switching from December to March contracts. When the December futures contract expires, the investor will want to consider what is the right price to trade the March contract, given the dividends that will occur and the interest that could be earned between December and March. The "Simple Forward Yield" of 5.73 percent is the benchmark yield because it is the forward rate between the December and the March expiration. The implied yield ("Roll Yield") in the calendar spread (buying December futures and selling March futures) is 5.78 percent, so the calendar spread on November 3, 1997, was close to being fairly valued for the S&P 500.

Other futures contracts—such as the futures on the Russell 2000, the S&P MidCap 400, and the Nasdaq 100 indexes—have much larger mispricings in the nearby contract and calendar spread. The larger mispricings in the Russell 2000 occur because the stocks have bid–offer spreads that might be as wide as 150 basis points (bps). Thus, the cost of doing arbitrage has more slippage, and the mispricing range that occurs prior to the arbitrage that brings futures back to fair value is wider than for S&P 500 futures. The difference between the forward yield and the implied yield in the calendar spread for the Russell 2000 is 27 bps. Generally, the arbitrage process keeps the contract prices in line with the cost of trading the stocks.

Volume. In a developed futures market, the dollar volume of the underlying stocks is typically a fraction of the dollar amount that trades in index futures. **Figure 1** shows average trading volume for U.S. stock index futures versus NYSE trading volume and shows open interest. The NYSE trades about $120 of futures for every $100 of stocks that trade on the NYSE. The ratio of open interest to the amount of futures trading volume outstanding for the NYSE in the United States has for some time been about three to one (that is, unwinding all of the open positions would take three trading days). In a new market, the ratio might be different. For example, DJIA futures have a lot more trading activity than open interest. Accordingly, institutional use of DJIA futures for longer-term index replication is still low; most investors appear to use the contract for day trading.

The stock market and the futures market should be thought of as parts of a complete market, but in the derivatives markets, the daily trading volume relative to open interest is a lot higher than within equities. On any given trading day, only 0.4 percent of the outstanding equities trade on the NYSE, so a small change in the information set or investors' risk preferences can create significant trading demands. If 0.8 percent or 0.9 percent of outstanding capitalization suddenly trades in a day instead of 0.4 percent, that increase can easily double NYSE volume and create a lot of market pressure.

Global derivatives applications are an interesting and growing area of the derivatives market. Futures activity has been growing relative to equity market activity in continental Europe and in Japan but falling slightly in the United States, the United Kingdom, and Hong Kong. **Table 2** shows the level of futures and options volume relative to stock market volume in major equity markets around the

Figure 1. Open Interest and Average Daily Volume for U.S. Stock Index Futures versus NYSE Daily Volume, April 1982–June 1997

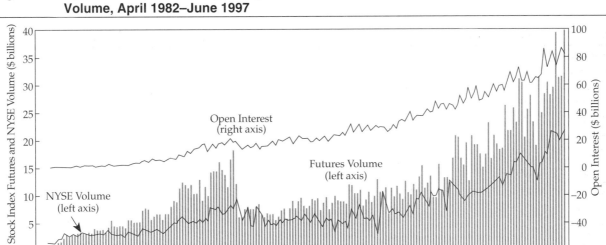

Table 2. Ratio of Futures and Options Volume to Stock Volume, as of December 31, 1997

Country	Futures/Stocks	Options/Stocks
United States	1.20	1.08
Canada	0.12	0.04
Japan	1.93	0.92
Hong Kong	0.75	0.24
Australia	0.99	0.30
United Kingdom	0.85	0.70
France	3.39	1.54
Germany	1.77	0.84
Switzerland	1.54	0.62
Netherlands	0.81	1.25
Spain	1.56	0.40
Italy	2.73	0.62
Sweden	0.36	0.66

world. In most cases, the notional amount that futures trade is half to one-and-a-half times the amount that stocks trade.

Cost Advantages. The way in which derivatives add value to global applications has much to do with the trading costs of stocks versus the trading costs of futures. **Table 3** reports estimates of trading costs for stocks and futures. The data are conservative; actual costs are often lower than shown. After accounting for taxes, commissions, market impact, and the need to roll the futures position, futures typically cost 10–20 percent of the round-trip cost to trade equities in most of the major markets. Futures will be less costly to trade than the equities, especially for an investor who wants index exposure for a year or less. This cost advantage is one of the reasons derivatives are used for equitizing cash and tactical domestic and global asset allocations, as well as for managing long and short equity exposure over short time periods.

Options

Most option strategies produce asymmetrical return payoffs. The value of an option is directly related to the underlying security's price. But value remains independent of judgments about the direction of the underlying stock price. Option-pricing models formalize the relationship between the variables that influence option pricing. In addition to option models, investors need to consider the impact of volatility on option prices, hedging interest, and the role of OTC options.

Pricing Models. Option-pricing models come primarily in two flavors: Black–Scholes models and Cox–Ross–Rubinstein models. Black–Scholes models use a continuous time approach with differential equations, and they work fine for most European options, which allow exercise only at expiration. Cox–Ross–Rubinstein models use a discrete time approach, use binomial trees, and are critical for American or any options that allow for early exercise during the life of the option. Despite the imperfections of the Black–Scholes model, it is probably still the basis for most option modeling, especially in equities.

Volatility. A key element of option-pricing models is that expected volatility increases the value of an option. In November 1997, expectations for higher volatility raised option premiums; index options are the most widely affected by increases in volatility. Investors use implied volatility derived from quoted option prices for comparing options much as they use bond yields to compare bonds. Investors cannot easily compare the prices of bonds of different maturities, so they use yields as a common measurement.

Table 3. Round-Trip Comparative Costs of Trading Stocks and Futures, as of December 1997

Cost Factor	United States	Japan	United Kingdom	France	Germany	Hong Kong
Stocks						
Commissions	0.12%	0.20%	0.20%	0.25%	0.25%	0.50%
Market impact[a]	0.30	0.70	0.70	0.50	0.50	0.50
Taxes	0.00	0.21	0.50	0.00	0.00	0.34
Total	0.42%	1.11%	1.40%	0.75%	0.75%	1.34%
Futures						
Commissions	0.01%	0.05%	0.02%	0.03%	0.02%	0.05%
Market impact[a]	0.05	0.10	0.10	0.10	0.10	0.10
Taxes	0.00	0.00	0.00	0.00	0.00	0.00
Total	0.06%	0.15%	0.12%	0.13%	0.12%	0.15%
Futures as percentage of stocks	14.28	13.51	8.60	17.00	16.00	11.19

Note: Assumes a $25 million cap-weighted indexed portfolio executed as agent and does not include settlement and custody fees. Local indexes: S&P 500, Nikkei 225, FTSE 100, CAC 40, DAX. All contracts except the CAC 40 are quarterly.

[a]Trader estimates.

Options are available on a stock or index with many different expirations and strike prices, and implied volatility is the common denominator. Investors back out implied volatility from option prices similarly to the way they back out bond yields from bond prices. In determining whether an option is rich or cheap, the reference point is how its implied volatility measures relative to the historical volatility of the stock or index. Also, implied volatility moves in trends or cycles in much the same way yields do. It exhibits a pattern of rising or falling levels over several weeks at a time with only minor reversals.

Volatility, like bond yields, also has a term structure. As **Figure 2** shows, implied volatility changes over time and often very quickly. On October 24, 1997, before the 7 percent market decline on October 27, implied volatility was about 21 percent and had a slight upward slope (short-term volatility was less than long-term volatility). The stock market decline followed by a reversal was hard for traders to deal with because they had to readjust their hedges, both in the decline and the rise. Consequently, S&P 500 Index option prices significantly increased, to about 30 percent implied volatility.

Hedging Interest. Prices of options (implied volatility versus historical volatility) have responded quickly to increased hedging interest, especially in the past two years since overwriting lost popularity. Historically, stock volatility in the U.S. market has been about 20 percent, but **Figure 3** shows that for the 1993–97 period, volatility was 8–9 percent, which was

highly unusual. Note that as historical volatility increases, implied volatility moves right with it. If option traders need to hedge a lot of their option positions, however, and the only people in the marketplace are the volatility buyers (that is, option buyers), implied volatility will move much higher than historical volatility because the option traders take on greater risk when all the buyers are short volatility. The same happens in a stock when a lot of people want to buy calls, especially around earnings announcements. As **Figure 4** shows, in late 1997, compensation (premiums) was available for people who wanted to sell calls and sell puts, because market makers were limited in the capital they could apply to selling options. Derivatives market participants follow the relationship between implied and historical volatility to measure the attractiveness of being long or short options—that is, long or short volatility.

OTC Options. OTC options are privately negotiated option contracts between two parties that agree on the underlying stock, stock portfolio, or index, as well as the strike price, expiration, and exercise style. The purpose of most OTC options is to extend the life of an existing option, have a different expiration date, work with a customized basket of underlying stocks, or maintain the confidentiality of a large transaction by executing it with a dealer.

OTC options fill gaps in listed derivatives trading. They might provide access to a market in which the dealer is an active participant but to which the client has limited access. Trading Swiss equity deri-

Figure 2. Term Structure of Volatility for S&P 500 Index Options, October 1997

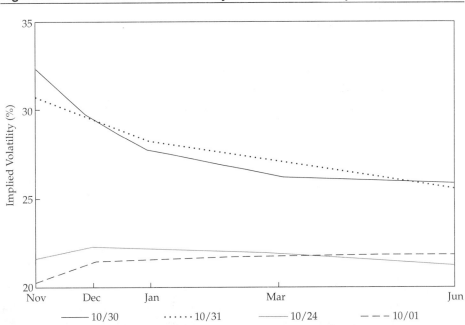

Figure 3.   Historical S&P 500 Volatility versus Implied Volatility of At-the-Money S&P 500 Option

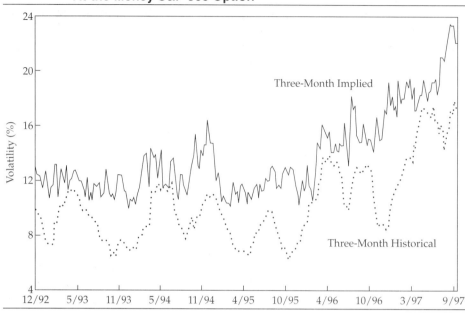

Figure 4.   Volatility Spread versus Change in S&P 500 Return

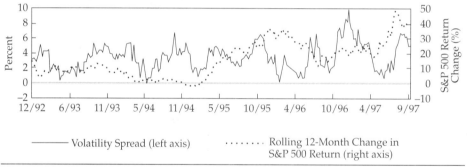

Note: Weekly through September 30, 1997.

vates OTC is a good example. U.S. institutions that want to buy futures on the Swiss Market Index cannot directly make that transaction. Such a transaction does not have Commodities Futures Trading Commission (CFTC) approval. To buy the Swiss market via derivatives, certain U.S. institutions can buy OTC call options from a dealer; the combination of a long call with a short put at the same strike price provides put–call parity, which is like owning the underlying index. The dealers, in turn, can hedge their option positions by selling the futures.

OTC options allow large-scale confidential block trading of index exposures or relative exposures. This aspect is especially helpful in implementing large-scale stock option or index option trades. The prices of OTC options can be based on where the dealer executes the hedge for the OTC option position on the dealer's book. Clients who have the flexibility to work the option trade over the course of a day or two

thus have the opportunity to minimize market impact of the transaction by making it less obvious to the public's eye.

Conditions Affecting Derivatives Activity

Volatility and market direction, the arrival of macroeconomic informations, and the regulatory environment are the primary influences on the level of derivatives activity globally.

Volatility and Market Direction. One reason derivatives are blamed for rising volatility is that people frequently want to adjust their index exposures when prices move, so trading in derivatives increases as markets become more volatile. This observation is especially true in the United States because U.S. investors tend to use derivatives to reduce risk rather than increase it. The greater the volatility, the more investors want to reduce their risk.

Restrictions on short selling are another reason for the growth in derivatives. Investors that cannot short stocks will instead trade futures or buy puts in declining markets. In places such as Taiwan and South Korea, swaps and futures are used to short the equity markets because the stock loan markets are not developed enough to allow short positions in stocks.

Information. Because most equity derivatives are index based, trading activity increases with the arrival of macroeconomic information. For an individual stock earnings announcement, investors might want to trade with a stock option. Many derivatives applications are part of top-down approaches, so the occurrence of a macro event increases trading activity.

Regulatory Environment. The regulatory environment also influences the amount and types of derivatives used. For example, investors in Europe are more comfortable with dealer-based markets, so OTC options are more commonly used in Europe, whereas exchange-traded options are favored in the United States. Also, some countries have prohibitions on the use of derivatives by certain people. For example, the CFTC must approve the use of futures by U.S. investors, so U.S. institutions can trade exchange-traded futures directly only in certain markets.

Liquidity Perspective

The liquidity of index futures contracts around the world is often superior to that of stocks. Futures trade on 90 percent of the capitalization of global equity indexes and 82 percent of the capitalization of world indexes that exclude the United States (MSCI's Europe/Australasia/Far East [EAFE] Index, for example). A total of about $48 billion in stocks trades each day in the world, and the total for futures is about 20 percent greater, approximately $59 billion. As **Table 4** shows, the United States accounts for more than half of global derivatives activity. In Germany, the derivatives market is important; Germany represents 9 percent of global futures volume but only 7 percent of global equities volume. Japan and Germany are, respectively, the bellwether derivatives markets for the Pacific and European regions. In the United Kingdom, derivatives use has not prospered because arbitrage is complicated by a lack of efficient convergence of futures to stock prices at expiration.

The United States dominates global listed options markets with about 71 percent of the total average daily options trading volume of $45 billion. The actual percentage of daily trading is higher when OTC options are also considered. Markets outside the

Table 4. Liquidity Perspective: Percentage of Global Trading in Listed Equity Index Derivatives, December 31, 1997

Country	Stocks	Futures	Options
Australia	1%	1%	0%
France	1	3	2
Germany	7	9	6
Hong Kong	6	3	2
Japan	7	11	7
Other Asia	2	1	—
Other Europe	9	9	7
United Kingdom	7	5	5
United States	60	57	71

United States, however, make more use of OTC options than listed index options.

With the liquidity in the futures and options markets, investors can set up synthetic index funds or use futures for global country allocation strategies. For example, if a large pension fund plans to hire portfolio managers next year to manage a $1 billion global equity portfolio and starts shifting and increasing international investment, the fund managers may prefer to create this exposure now and then unwind it as they hire managers. They need to know which markets have enough liquidity to handle a $1 billion position. Another investor might want to implement a global asset allocation strategy and need to trade $100 million in a shift. **Table 5** shows the percentage of a day's volume and the percentage of a day's open interest affected by setting up a $1 billion synthetic index fund globally or doing a $100 million trade in these markets. With a few exceptions, a $1 billion synthetic index fund represents a small fraction of daily trading activity and open interest. In the major options and futures markets, $100 million is less than 10 percent of a day's volume and a very small percentage of open interest. For smaller European markets, a shift of $100 million would begin to absorb significant liquidity, but for most large markets, it is a modest trade.

Note that, although the Canadian market has grown significantly from what it was several years ago, it still reports less activity in listed derivatives than some of the other major global markets. Hong Kong and Italy are also doing more and more business in derivatives, although they are not in the top group.

As **Table 6** shows, the notional amount of futures contracts is distributed along similar lines as market capitalization, except that Germany has a much larger derivatives presence than its capitalization would suggest. Germany has 11 percent of global open interest, but its equity market has only 4 percent of global market cap.

Table 5. Liquidity of the Futures Market

Country	Index	Weight	Global Synthetic Index Fund ($1 billion)		Global Asset Allocation ($100 million)		Average Daily Volume ($ millions)	Average Open Interest ($ millions)
			Daily Volume	Daily Open Interest	Daily Volume	Daily Open Interest		
United States	S&P 500	52.93%	1.5%	0.6%	0.3%	0.1%	31,591	86,547
Japan[a]	TOPIX	11.98	10.1	0.9	8.4	0.7	1,191	13,512
	Nikkei 225	—	2.9	0.4	2.4	0.3	4,113	32,684
United Kingdom	FTSE 100	10.99	3.9	0.8	3.6	0.7	2,791	13,795
Germany	DAX	4.02	0.7	0.2	1.8	0.4	5,636	25,968
France	CAC 40	3.40	1.5	0.5	4.4	1.5	2,257	6,700
Switzerland	SMI	3.19	2.5	0.6	7.8	2.0	1,282	4,900
Canada	TSE 35	2.48	16.5	1.1	66.6	4.4	150	2,293
Netherlands	AEX	2.41	2.8	0.7	11.7	2.8	854	3,577
Italy	MIB 30	1.67	0.8	0.5	4.7	3.2	2,144	3,116
Hong Kong	Hang Seng	1.56	0.7	0.3	4.7	2.1	2,127	4,729
Sweden	OMX	1.38	6.1	1.7	44.1	12.3	227	814
Australia	All Ords	1.41	2.4	0.2	18.5	1.7	542	5,976
Spain	IBEX 35	1.17	1.2	0.5	9.	4.2	1,020	2,390
Belgium	BEL	0.71	5.2	1.3	72.9	17.9	137	559
Denmark	KFX	0.36	15.7	3.2	549.2	113.6	18	88
Malaysia	KLCI	0.50	15.9	5.2	398.6	129.5	25	77
Austria	ATX	0.15	6.3	0.4	433.0	28.9	23	345

Note: Weights based on December 31, 1997, Financial Times/S&P Actuaries World Index capitalizations. Volume and open interest as of same date.
[a]Weight for Japan combines weights for TOPIX and Nikkei 225.

Table 6. Market Capitalization and Open Interest in Listed Equity Index Derivatives, December 31, 1997
(percent of world)

Country	Market Capitalization	Open Interest
Australia	1%	3%
France	3	3
Germany	4	11
Hong Kong	2	2
Japan	12	26
Other Asia	0	—
Other Europe	12	7
United Kingdom	11	6
United States	55	42

Derivative Strategies

Derivative products are effective tools that can make existing strategies more efficient or can make new strategies possible. They have four general areas of application: efficient/enhanced fund management, asset allocation, active or view-driven strategies, and risk management.

Enhanced Fund Management. Efficient or enhanced fund management strategies include using futures to equitize cash, tightening benchmark tracking with overlays, futures-related portfolio trading to keep costs down, enhancing returns from cheap futures, cash management or market-neutral strategies, and synthetic international indexing.

▦ *Equitizing cash.* Futures provide an efficient way to maintain strategic asset-class weights, or a fully invested position. Equitizing cash appeals to investors who require ways to keep cash invested to minimize the unintended risk of the cash flows in positions. This application, using futures to equitize cash or carry an ongoing position of cash in a mutual fund to provide room for withdrawals, is probably the most basic and widely used application of equity derivatives. Investment managers can experience problems with intermittent cash flows caused by money inflows or, worse, large withdrawals in a short period of time, which force the manager to sell stocks.

The cost in basis points of carrying cash increases as a portfolio's cash allocation increases and as equity market returns increase. As **Figure 5** shows, with a cash allocation of 8 percent, the cost of carrying cash is considerably higher when equity market returns are 25 percent than when returns are 6 percent—2.0 percent per year versus 0.4 percent.

To create the synthetic index (benchmark) exposure, the investor simply buys a quantity of contracts based on the amount of cash to be invested divided by the notional value of each contact (Index × Multiplier). For benchmarks with no futures contracts, such as the Russell 1000, a combination of other index futures (e.g., the S&P 500 and the S&P MidCap) can be determined that will track the benchmark as closely as possible. Precise determination of the number of contracts involves adjusting for the interest rate sensitivity of daily realized gains and losses, which is sometimes called "tailing the hedge."

▦ *Tightening benchmark tracking.* Benchmark tracking is a big concern because performance measurement is increasingly tied to benchmarks.

Figure 5. Using Futures to Equitize Cash

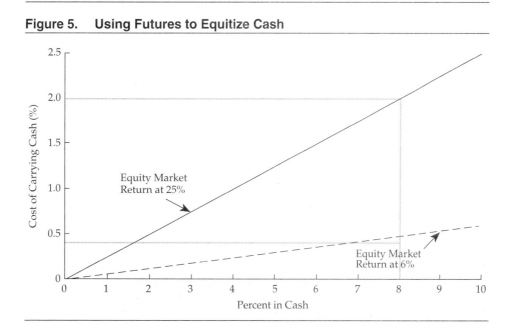

Managers also worry about tracking benchmarks because their compensation is often performance based. The solution is a simple exercise: For however much cash is taken in, the manager buys a basket of futures to mimic the benchmark for the existing portfolio holding. The manager might construct a portfolio of DJIA futures, Nasdaq 100 futures, S&P 500 futures—whatever benchmark or mix of benchmarks has the most similarity to the actual holding. For every $1 million the manager takes in, the manager simply buys $1 million worth of that basket of futures. This approach quickly and efficiently achieves exposure to the required benchmark.

■ *Futures-related trading.* Certain types of portfolio trades tap into the liquidity or ease of dealer hedging from the availability of futures. Portfolio managers can lower stock-trading costs through futures-related trades. The two most commonly used futures-related trades are exchange-for-physical (EFP) trades and basis trades. Futures-related trades are most commonly used when a portfolio has 5 percent or less of tracking error with an index or a portfolio of index futures, although the tracking error could be as high as 7 percent or even more. The trade is much cheaper than trading stocks in a traditional manner because it takes advantage of the fact that the dealer can hedge in the derivatives market.

In a typical EFP trade, a fund manager exchanges portfolios for futures (or vice versa) at a spread negotiated as a markup or a markdown to the fair value of the future. Stocks are exchanged at opening or closing prices adjusted for the spread. The cost is generally about 1 cent per share—a little less for selling stock and buying futures, a little more for the other side. This 1 cent cost applies to a portfolio that is exactly like the S&P 500; for something that has, say, a 3 percent tracking error with the S&P 500, the price would include a risk premium, so the cost of tracking would be higher. Basically, the dealer at the end of that transaction is long futures/short stocks—or the other way around. This approach is well suited to transition management and takes advantage of a natural hedge to the dealer. It is also a much cheaper way of trading than when a market maker is needed to make a market in individual stocks.

In a basis trade, a portfolio is exchanged for cash, again at a spread negotiated with the dealer. Clients who want to buy stocks ask the dealer to quote a price for giving them the particular stock portfolio as a basis trade. The dealer who wins buys futures over the course of the day, with the timing often directed by the client. Then, based on the average futures price the dealer paid and the negotiated spread, the dealer sells that portfolio to the client. The client never directly takes on a futures position but can take advantage of the fact that the dealer is putting on the

hedge in the course of the trading day for the commitment to give the fund manager the portfolio at the end of the day.

■ *Enhanced equity returns with derivatives.* Most investors earn their return enhancement from managing the cash available when they establish a long position via futures. One approach is for investors to buy a cash-equivalent (money market) portfolio, invest the dollar amount in a U.S. or international index futures contract, and within the cash-equivalent portfolio, pursue some active strategies that add alpha (excess return). Instead of getting their alpha from stock picking, they get it from cash management or structured fixed-income products. Another approach is to use market-neutral strategies, such as long/short or volatility trading.

One of the ways managers can obtain alpha is from cheap futures. "Cheap" futures trade below their fair value when financing costs and expected dividends are considered. As **Figure 6** shows, since 1982, the deviation of the nearby S&P 500 futures contract from fair value has historically followed a regular pattern that rarely goes beyond 0.5 percent rich or cheap per month. As **Figure 7** shows, S&P 500 futures tend to trade below fair value on days when the index declines more than one standard deviation. Only in extreme markets is a similar tendency toward richness found. Thus, declining markets often lead to cheap futures; if the market is falling, an investor has an opportunity to find some excess return.

Futures will move away from fair value for the following reasons:
* *Arbitrage.* Arbitrage costs will drive the mispricing that investors observe in the marketplace at any time for a futures contract, but other factors are probably more important.
* *Dividend treatment.* In some markets, different groups of investors get different dividend treatment. Most foreign stocks have 15 percent of their dividends withheld for tax purposes. In local European markets, some investors receive dividend tax credits. Futures typically price off of the tax treatment of the local investor. For example, in Germany, the local investor gets 120–140 percent of a quoted dividend yield. Futures in Germany and similar markets trade very cheaply during dividend season. So, investors in the United States, who get 85 percent of German dividends, find advantages in the second quarter of the year to owning German equities via futures. This pattern occurs because domestic investors in Germany have the incentive to buy stocks, receive dividend tax credits, and short futures.

Figure 8 shows the cheapness of the German futures depicted in the calendar spread. In the first quarter of each year, the futures trades were

Figure 6. S&P 500 Nearby Futures Contract: Deviation from Fair Value, June 1982–August 1997

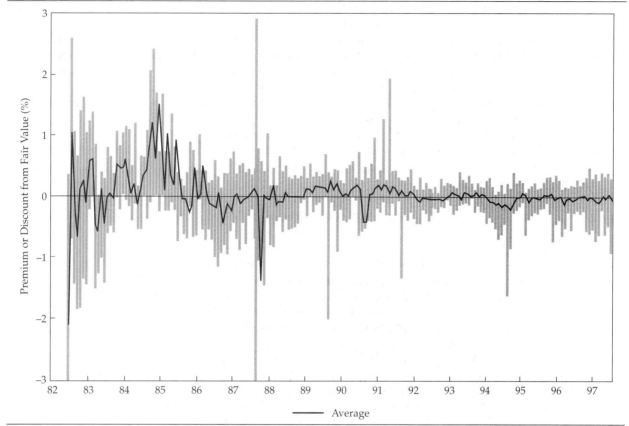

Note: The actual low for June 1982 was –4.139 percent; for October 1987, –10.07 percent.

noticeably below fair value. This regular pattern results from an implied dividend yield in the future, which is usually about 125 percent of the dividend during this period. This pattern also happens in France and Italy. At Goldman Sachs, we have clients who swap out of their German and French stocks during that period and buy the futures contract to take advantage of this pattern. Lending the stocks is more commonplace than swapping; the returns to lending stocks during this period also reflect this pattern.

- *Convergence rules.*
- *Demand for liquidity when a major market trend emerges.* Demand for liquidity when a major market trend emerges is certainly a reason for futures misvaluation. For example, in late 1997, in Taiwan and Malaysia as indexes declined sharply, futures sold between 500 and 1,000 bps cheap. If an investor wants to buy those markets, a swap or a future can provide an alpha between 500 and 1,000 bps, but the investor has to accept the stocks that are in that index.
- *Effect on costs of ability to sell short.* Restrictions on short selling tend to contribute to cheapness in futures prices because selling futures acts as a

substitute for short selling. Investors are willing to sell futures below fair value because they have no other way of creating a short market position.

- *Newness of market.*
- *Investor strategy preference.*

Investors running an enhanced index fund or equitizing cash with futures may find that they need to trade the calendar spread and roll their positions (exchange an expiring futures contract for one farther from expiration). The cost at which they roll positions is related to interest rates because the attractiveness of stocks relative to fixed-income alternatives is a key factor for top-down investors who use futures to manage equity exposure. Annual mispricing in the S&P 500 futures calendar spread moves in cycles and, as **Figure 9** shows, has been inversely related to the level of interest rates. During most of 1997 and early 1998, the annualized cost of rolling positions was 5–10 bps above the index for investors earning LIBOR deposit yields on short-term cash investments. From the perspective of investors buying synthetic equity exposure with futures, richness in the calendar spread represents index underperformance and cheapness generates a positive alpha. Since 1994, futures mispricing has been modest,

Figure 7. Changes in Futures Mispricing Compared with Index Changes, December 31, 1995, to June 20, 1997

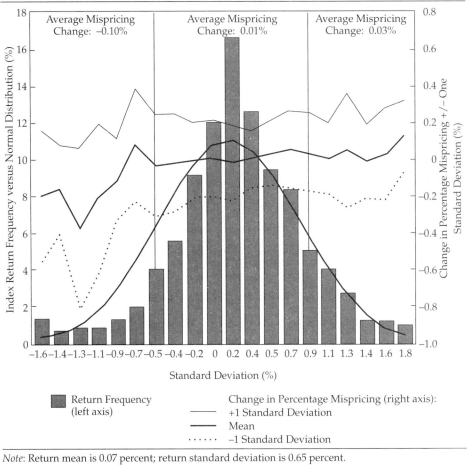

Note: Return mean is 0.07 percent; return standard deviation is 0.65 percent.

within the range of plus or minus 30 bps a year. Periods of significant richness and cheapness tend to persist for several quarters when they occur and make running enhanced index funds unattractive unless the investor gets a lot of alpha from fixed income. The quarterly returns of a benchmark synthetic S&P 500 Index fund for managers who equitize cash or practice synthetic index investing for 1992 through 1997 are shown in **Table 7**. The annualized monthly return tracking error over the last three years has been about 1.2 percent, but much of this tracking error is noise, as indicated by the much smaller annual return differences shown in Table 7.

Return differences from S&P 500 Index results on a monthly basis have recently become larger but are typically plus or minus 40 bps. As **Figure 10** shows, wide swings in one month tend to be reversed the next month (measured over the period, the correlation of these differences was –0.55).

Alternative cash management strategies. Cash held in synthetic index funds can be invested in short-term securities or other market-neutral strategies. The alpha from these strategies (returns in

excess of LIBOR) can be "transported" to the asset class underlying the future or swap. Within the short-term fixed-income management arena, managers who run enhanced index funds, domestically or internationally, take on yield-curve risk by extending maturities, assume credit risk, or use mortgage-backed securities with elements of credit and prepayment risk to enhance yield.

Table 7. S&P 500 versus Synthetic Index Fund

Period	S&P 500	Synthetic Index Fund	Difference
1992	7.61%	7.69%	0.08%
1993	10.06	9.38	–0.68
1994	1.31	1.28	–0.03
1995	37.53	37.54	–0.01
1996	22.95	22.63	–0.32
1997	33.35	33.45	0.10
Tracking error (five years annualized)		1.040%	
Tracking error (three years annualized)		1.239	

Figure 8. DAX Calendar Spread Mispricing: January 1, 1996, to October 31, 1997

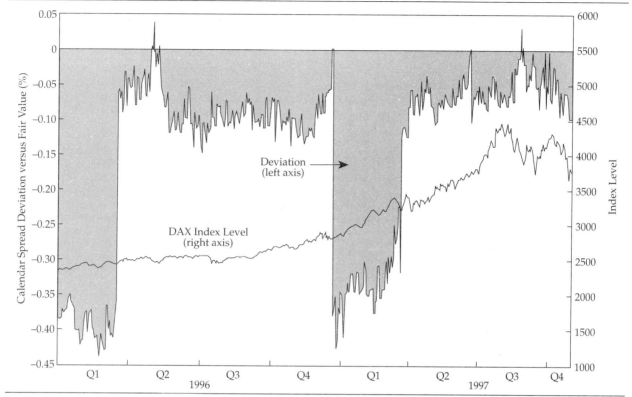

Equity-based synthetic index strategies include the following:

- *Long/short stock strategies.* Buy (sell) the most (least) attractive stocks while holding the dollar amount of long/short positions in balance.
- *Hybrid bond arbitrage.* Buy a convertible or structured note and create an offsetting position by shorting stock, selling a call, or buying a put.
- *Option volatility trades.* Construct long and short positions in index, fixed-income, or currency options to benefit from moves in absolute or relative implied volatility.

Of these alternatives, volatility strategies are somewhat easier to unwind or modify because of the greater liquidity of the instruments used and because tracking error can be kept under 2 percent. The horizon over which the results will be realized is shorter with volatility trades. Stock (or convertible bond) long/short strategies tend to have slightly higher tracking risk–reward trade-offs.

■ *Synthetic international indexing.* The use of derivatives for international investing expedites the investment process for active and passive international managers. International equity derivatives are currently of great interest because international investing has grown and because trading in international markets has a relatively high cost. Many active U.S. managers now have discretion to allocate as much as 10 percent of their portfolio to international markets.

The primary use of derivatives in international investing is to provide a low-cost method of managing country exposure. The costs of trading stocks internationally are much higher than the costs of trading futures. Table 3 showed a sample of trading costs for futures versus stocks in six major global equity markets.

In addition, derivatives provide a natural separation of equity and currency exposure, in the sense that investors can put cash equivalents in dollar-based instruments and get the desired liquidity. For example, if an investor buys a portfolio that replicates the Financial Times/S&P Actuaries World Index (FT/S&P-AWI) EuroPac or the EAFE Index, the investor has a synthetic currency-hedged investment in international markets. To create a position in, say, Japanese equities, an investor who owns U.S. dollar money market securities and buys Nikkei 225 futures must also buy the yen forward to achieve yen exposure. Otherwise, the investor has, in effect, a hedged currency exposure, except for the gains/losses that accumulate in that Nikkei 225 position.

Another advantage derivatives provide is that they can capture the full dividend—and sometimes more—by avoiding dividend withholding taxes that are incurred in stock holdings.

Finally, international exposure through derivatives takes advantage of the liquidity and operational efficiencies in the derivatives markets.

Figure 9. S&P 500 Futures Calendar Spread (Implied Yield minus Eurodollar Futures Yield) versus 30-Year U.S. T-Bond Rate

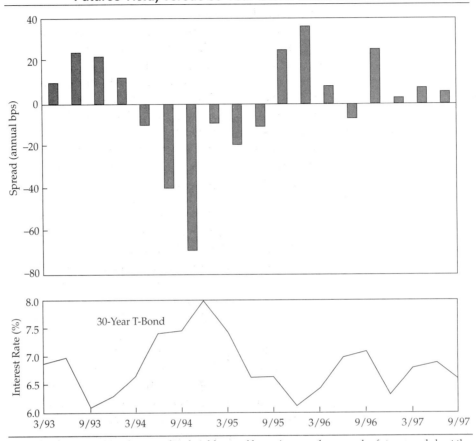

Note: The implied yield is the annualized yield earned by an investor long nearby futures and short the future expiring three months later. Index and T-bond levels taken on the last business day of the month prior to expiration.

Figure 10. Difference between Synthetic S&P 500 Index and S&P 500 Total Returns

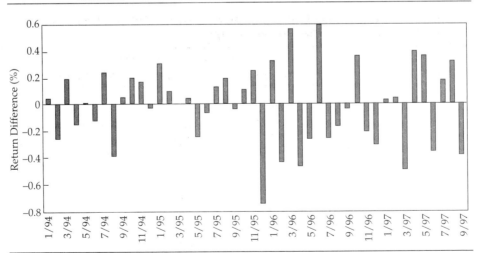

Despite their benefits, derivatives complement stock selection; they are not a replacement for it. International derivatives applications do have their drawbacks and limitations. For example, using deriv-atives in international investing forces investors to deal with the futures indexes (the indexes on which futures are based); exposure is based on futures indexes. Futures are usually based on exchange indexes that have a long history—such as the German DAX Index, French CAC 40 Index, and Tokyo Price Index (TOPIX)—or a narrower base of more-liquid stocks, as in most European futures indexes. Some of these indexes have limited coverage, so portfolio managers must be equipped to trade and monitor overlay positions.

Differences in coverage from benchmark indexes create tracking error and can create annual return spreads from benchmark indexes of as much as 3–4 percent. A synthetic global portfolio using a basket of country equity index futures can diversify some of this tracking risk so that deviations from benchmarks are 1–2 percent, depending on the number of futures in the portfolio. **Table 8** contains estimates of tracking error from BARRA's Global Equity Model and shows how closely an investor can track the FT/S&P-AWI EuroPac using various country combinations of futures contracts. If an investor used nine CFTC-approved contracts, the tracking error is higher than if 11 different futures contracts were used—1.50 percent versus 0.70 percent.

In addition to tracking error, performance measurement and attribution in overlay or synthetic country allocation are somewhat complicated. **Table 9** provides a summary of performance components that affect returns from synthetic index exposure. Futures may require holding excess cash for posting variation margin, which also can put a slight drag on performance. To separate the most important of these effects, users of futures for managing country expo-

sure may wish to measure performance relative to a basket of futures indexes as well as benchmark country indexes.

Using international derivatives places incremental financial and administrative burdens on portfolio managers and firms, not unlike developing a new product or strategy. Firms must have processes, procedures, and clear guidelines in place for monitoring exposure and capital at risk. Firms must keep in mind that certain clients may have restrictions on derivatives use. International index derivatives require ongoing management for rolling positions as futures expire and for keeping currency exposure in place as well as for managing the cash representing the notional amount of the index exposure. Moving from domestic to international derivatives also means changing from managing S&P 500 futures to managing a portfolio of as many as 11 futures in international markets, some of which expire at different times (many of them expire monthly). Such a task requires extensive trading and settlement resources.

Swaps are an alternative to futures, with many common features that firms may find more useful for synthetic investing in emerging markets.

Because of the international markets' volatility, many investors will want to do their own due diligence on these markets—visit the exchanges to understand the clearing mechanisms and verify for themselves that the safeguards are in place.

In short, international investing with derivatives offers flexibility and lower trading costs but also has

Table 8. Synthetic International Index Fund Allocation Analysis: Futures Baskets Designed to Track FT/S&P-AWI EuroPac, as of December 31, 1997

Region/Country	Futures Index	FT Weight	Futures Optimized Weight as Percentage of Basket			
			11 Contracts	10 Contracts	9 CFTC Contracts	8 CFTC Contracts
Pacific						
Japan	TOPIX	26.12%	27.08%	27.31%	28.13%	28.44%
Hong Kong	Hang Seng	3.40	3.82	3.95	3.87	4.03
Australia	All Ords	2.79	3.76	3.94	4.02	4.25
Subtotal		32.31%	34.66%	35.20%	36.02%	36.72%
Europe						
United Kingdom	FTSE 100	23.96%	24.45%	24.91%	29.68%	30.40%
Germany	DAX	8.75	9.33	9.15	13.77	13.64
France	CAC 40	7.410	7.70	8.18	9.63	10.30
Switzerland	SMI	6.94	7.09	7.33	—	—
Netherlands	EOE	5.25	6.96	6.97	—	—
Italy	MIB 30	3.65	3.91	4.39	3.92	4.54
Sweden	OMX	3.00	3.40	3.87	3.78	4.40
Spain	IBEX 35	2.58	2.50	—	3.20	—
Subtotal		61.54%	65.35%	64.81%	63.99%	63.29%
Total		93.85%	100.00%	100.00%	100.00%	100.00%
BARRA annualized tracking error			0.70%	0.80%	1.50%	1.58%

Table 9. Optimal Synthetic Index Exposure: Performance Components

±	Tracking error
	    Countries used
	    Country local indexes versus benchmark indexes

±	Cost/benefits of rolling futures
±	Futures mispricing cost/benefit
±	Return on cash and currency management
+	Trading cost savings
+	Tax effects of dividend versus interest income
+	Stock custody and clearing charges
–	No returns from lending stocks

a lot of moving parts—tracking error and other drawbacks that should be weighed against the trading cost savings and other advantages—so investors should gain an understanding of the expertise and resources required prior to strategy implementation.

Asset Allocation. Derivatives can be used to accomplish virtually any asset allocation strategy for domestic, international, and global portfolios. In an international setting, derivative applications include implementing decisions about country allocation and using options in tactical asset allocation (TAA) strategies, equity swaps, and equity-linked notes.

■ *Country allocation.* To comprehend the flexibility of derivatives in international asset allocation, consider how efficiently a portfolio manager can implement asset allocation shifts between countries using stock index futures and currency forwards. For example, suppose you are the manager of a $100 million portfolio that emphasizes your ability to allocate country equities and you want to change the portfolio's existing country weightings. **Table 10** outlines the existing weightings and desired weightings

for each country and indicates the required derivative transactions to implement the entire rebalancing.

In this case, you want to reduce allocations to Japan and Germany; increase allocations to the United Kingdom, France, and Hong Kong; and keep Switzerland steady. In this hypothetical international application, if you sell $10 million of TOPIX against an EAFE portfolio, you get a hedged Japanese equity position or synthetic cash earning the yen/dollar rate. Then, you must also sell the yen forward to eliminate the Japanese currency risk. Next, you could buy stock index futures and the currencies of the countries or markets in which you want to increase exposure. This shift is an example of a global asset allocation that can be implemented quickly and efficiently with derivatives.

■ *TAA options strategies.* Another application of derivatives for asset allocation is using options in TAA strategies. Many TAA strategies involve a commitment to sell if the market moves higher and to buy if it moves lower. This contingent trade is similar to selling a call option or put option against a portfolio. Some strategies that use TAA have incorporated selling calls and selling puts at points where trading is likely. The advantage of this arrangement is that if the trading point is not reached, the investor keeps the premium income. The benefit of the commitment to trade enables these strategies to perform better when the market is expected to remain in a trading range. This strategy is definitely attractive, but although some investors use it when option volatility is high, the strategy has the possibility of locking investors into trading when the asset allocation process calls for different trades. For example, in trading stocks versus bonds, even though the investor is selling

Table 10. Implementing Country Allocation Decisions

A. Sample Portfolio

Country	Current Weighting	Desired Weighting	Change
Japan	30%	20%	–10%
United Kingdom	20	25	5
France	15	25	10
Germany	15	5	–10
Switzerland	10	10	0
Hong Kong	10	15	5

B. Transactions Required to Implement Entire Shift

Equities	Currencies
Sell $10 million of TOPIX	Sell $10 million of yen
Sell $10 million of DAX	Sell $10 million of German mark
Buy $5 million of FTSE 100	Buy $5 million of British pound
Buy $10 million of CAC 40	Buy $10 million of French franc
Buy $5 million of Hang Seng	Buy $5 million of Hong Kong dollar

stocks, if stock prices rise and bond prices rise farther than stock prices, bonds might be the first asset class the strategy reduces. If the investor is short an option committing him or her to the sale of stocks, the strategy could force a transaction in the wrong asset class.

■ *Equity swaps.* Swaps are another means of overlay investing or shorting of equity exposure. They represent a negotiated agreement between two parties to exchange capital or total returns for an interest payment at specific reset dates. Like futures, the notional amount of the investment is free to be invested in short-term fixed-income securities or market-neutral strategies. With swaps, the parties have potential credit risk exposure to each other between reset dates, but with futures, which are marked to market daily, the credit risk lasts only overnight and is with an exchange. Swaps can also be used in markets with no futures or as a way of trading in markets to which U.S. investors do not have easy access or have no access, such as Taiwan, Thailand, Korea, and Malaysia. Swaps are also used when the indexes on which futures trade cannot be combined to create the equity portfolio profile desired by the investor. These swaps, specified in terms of specific stocks, can be expensive unless the other side of the swap can be found. The swap level is struck where the dealer would trade the stock.

Specific swap applications include a substitute for futures in markets with no futures, two-sided exposure trading interest, gaining access to an equity market in the face of foreign ownership restrictions, leverage, and customized indexes.

- *Substitute for futures.* Swaps can be used in many of the same applications as futures. Swaps typically have a term of one year or more and, therefore, eliminate the need to roll futures; the expected costs and risks of rolling futures, however, are reflected in the swap cost or spread. From a trading cost perspective, investors consider substituting swaps for futures when they expect to have a position longer than a year and a half. In that case, the trading costs and the hassle of rolling the futures outweigh the incremental up-front cost of doing the swap.
- *Two-sided exposure trading interest.* A swap can be a win/win situation if two sides can be found and the dealer acts as intermediary. In some emerging markets in Asia, two-way trading interest is regular and swap markets are quite active.
- *Foreign ownership restrictions.* If an investor wants a long-term core position and cannot own stocks because of regulatory restrictions, swaps can achieve the desired exposure. For example, Canadian markets have restrictions on foreign

equity investments, so a Canadian investor could achieve long-term U.S. equity exposure by swapping the S&P 500 Index return (dividends and capital gains) for LIBOR plus a spread and keeping the cash in Canadian debt securities.

- *Leverage.* Swaps can provide leveraged exposure to a market for active trading accounts, such as hedge funds. Financing stock positions directly can be costly, and the stock must be held as collateral for the loan. Engaging in a return swap, such as receiving the return of the German DAX and paying the return of the Japanese TOPIX, is an efficient way of taking a position with cash flows restricted to quarterly reset dates.
- *Customized indexes.* Investors can achieve exposure to customized indexes using swaps. For example, an investor might want overlay exposure to an index or basket specific to a market view, such as bank stocks in Japan or "red chip" China stocks traded in Hong Kong.

■ *Equity-linked notes.* Equity-linked notes (ELNs) are securities that provide international equity exposure in a fixed-income format. The principal is protected, and the final principal payment amount is tied to the move in an index, sector, or basket of stocks. An ELN consists of a zero-coupon or low-coupon bond and a call option. In the case of a zero coupon, the difference between the discounted note price and par is used to buy a call option on an equity index, but the dividend return is usually not included in the final principal payment. Fund managers primarily use ELNs as a conservative means to equitize cash, gain timely and efficient access to international or emerging markets in a principal-protected format, and establish a core holding of equities.

Equity index participation rates in ELNs are typically 100 percent and above. The larger the amount of current income the investor desires, the smaller the equity participation. The investor typically pays par for the ELN, and higher current income raises the value of the fixed-income component of the structure and reduces the equity participation. ELNs are extremely flexible, and selected international structures can be tailored to remove the currency exchange risk.

Active or View-Driven Strategies. Investors who have an opinion on a stock, on a sector, or simply on market timing can implement their active strategies with derivatives. Many applications of single-stock or sector derivatives are based on active views. Derivatives applications include shifting market/benchmark exposure, short-term stock/sector call sales (bearish/neutral), volatility trading, and using a note with embedded single-stock exposure.

■ *Shifting market/benchmark exposure.* Investors can think of shifting exposure as shifting their beta to an industry, to an international market, or to a value or growth index. Derivatives provide several vehicles to alter existing exposure.

• *U.S. Index futures or swaps.* Futures or swaps on the S&P 500, S&P MidCap 400, DJIA, Nasdaq 100, or Russell 2000 provide moderate to high liquidity and enable investors to offset or create a small-cap bias by selling (buying) medium/small-cap futures and buying (selling) S&P 500 or DJIA futures.

• *International index futures or swaps.* Managers can reduce unwanted country benchmark risk as they pick stocks by using country index futures, which have good liquidity.

• *Value and growth futures or swaps.* An overemphasis or underemphasis on a style can be adjusted by using size and value or growth index futures. **Figure 11** shows the range of indexes for which an investor can use derivatives to adjust small-cap/large-cap and value/growth exposures; the mapping is according to the BARRA size and growth factors. An investor may not be able to do all the desired trades (large trades, $150 million a day, cannot be done in the Russell 2000 or

S&P MidCap). Because of liquidity constraints, investors can build a basket or a combination of these indexes to track most active portfolios.

• *Industry index options or swaps.* Gaps in industry coverage can be remedied with a basket of stocks or industry index derivatives. For example, a long call/short put position at the same strike price provides the same payoff as a basket of the underlying stocks—in effect, a forward on this basket. These strategies make sense for investors who have concerns about market risk, style, or sector weight and want to shift exposure for up to or less than one year.

■ *Short-term stock/sector call sales.* Industry and sector derivatives in the form of index options can be used to implement a research view on a particular industry or sector. A number of investment research departments, including Goldman Sachs', have focused their attention on industry perspectives or themes, and industry index options provide an easy way to implement their views. Leveraging views on the relative performance of specific securities within an industry is another use for options and swaps.

The use of derivatives to adjust exposure to particular stocks should be driven, first of all, by the

Figure 11. U.S. Futures Indexes Mapped on BARRA Size and Growth Factors

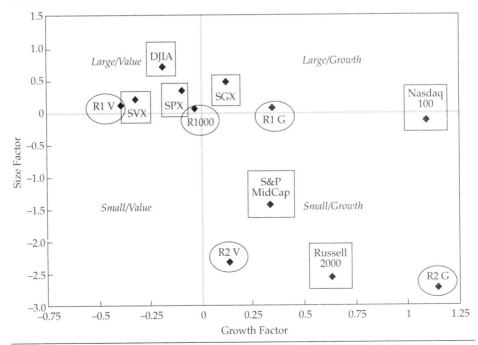

Note: R1 V = Russell 1000 Value Index
R1 G = Russell 1000 Growth Index
SVX = S&P Value Index

R2 V = Russell 2000 Value Index
R2 G = Russell 2000 Growth Index
SGX = S&P Growth Index
SPX = S&P 500 Index

Source: BARRA U.S. Equity Model, October 22, 1997.

investor's well-researched opinion of the stock and, second, by the pricing of the option on that stock. A stock option strategy should not be done simply because an option valuation screen turns up a name. The option strategy is secondary to the view on the stock. For example, in October 1997, the actual and implied volatility of semiconductor stocks increased and the stock of Applied Materials, a U.S.-based semiconductor equipment maker, suffered a decline in price that could have represented a buying opportunity. An investor with a bullish view on Applied Materials could have acquired a position at a reduced cost by committing to buy the stock through a put sale and capitalizing on a rise in the premium of the options because of the high implied volatility.

Selling calls is also a way of improving the income yield on stocks that have high volatility and no dividend yield. For example, investors might want to own a low-dividend company but want to transform the holding into something that has a lower risk profile. Instead of selling the stock, they can sell a call against a portion of the position and translate some of that potential capital gain into an income yield from the call sale. In a way, selling calls and receiving the premium is like trading off uncertain capital gains for an up-front substitute for dividend yield. If equity market returns move back to a more "normal" range, enhancing income by selling upside yields will be an important strategy in the application of derivatives in the future.

■ *Volatility trading.* Volatility trading is a new area that allows an investor to capitalize on a view that volatility will rise or fall. The trading can be done at the index or stock level. For example, after the Asian currency crisis in late 1997, implied volatility of index options rose sharply as investors implemented hedging trades and option market makers reacted to a more costly trading environment for keeping their trading books in balance. This development presented an opportunity for taking a view that the volatility premium in index options was excessive. Investors could have sold put spreads or call spreads with high sensitivity to a volatility decline to capitalize on the opportunity. Alternatively, they could have sold a "volatility swap," in which a dealer pays the investor a return based on the extent to which actual market volatility is below a "strike level" for the swap. The strike level is typically close to the implied volatility in options with the same term as the swap. The advantage of the swap structure is that the investor's payoff is based entirely on the realized volatility, which leaves the dealer with the task of managing the options position required to deliver the payoff.

Many companies exhibit a pattern of rising volatility just before an earnings announcement. An unusually sharp rise could indicate a greater degree of investor uncertainty. For example, prior to the September 16, 1997, earnings announcement for software provider Oracle Corporation, implied volatility of options on Oracle increased to 47 percent—almost 4 percent above its three-month average. For investors interested in taking advantage of increased volatility levels, selling call options could be attractive. If an investor had confidence in the earnings numbers coming out and was willing to sell the stock at a certain price, that investor could collect a fee from people who wanted to speculate. When Oracle was at $38, investors could sell a put option with a $40 strike for almost $1.875. (The day after the earnings announcement, Oracle dropped to $36.0625, and it remained below the $40 strike until expiration in October.)

■ *Notes with embedded single-stock exposure.* Applications of derivatives that provide investors downside protection are receiving increased interest lately. Of special interest are structured notes and synthetic convertible securities, which are alternatives to owning stocks that effectively supply a floor in declining price scenarios in exchange for fractional (less than full) participation in upside returns.

In summary, derivatives strategy should start with an investment view. Then, the investor should consider what the strategy or alternative strategies will do to beta, or equity exposure, and align that understanding with the investment view.

Risk Management. Portfolio managers and risk managers use modern portfolio theory as the framework within which they operate, but they have different objectives and use different tactics. The portfolio manager's objective is to find the best asset mix given the desired risk–return trade-off and the available investments, but the risk manager assesses the level and drivers of risk in the ongoing investment process. The portfolio manager estimates excess return and risk characteristics for a particular time horizon, but the risk manager measures and decomposes risk characteristics, focusing on the primary drivers of existing risks and their interrelationships.

Proper design of a hedging strategy starts with identifying the risk that needs to be hedged. This step often requires understanding the client's short-term view or concerns and any special constraints relevant to the client's situation. In general, the more narrow or specific the risk to be hedged, the more important that the characteristics of the hedging vehicle match the source of risk. **Exhibit 1** provides a summary of risks that may need to be hedged and possible hedging instruments. Once the type of risk is identified, the next step is to select an appropriate hedging instrument. This step often requires analyzing the

Exhibit 1. Identifying the Risk to Be Hedged

View or Situation	Type of Risk to Be Hedged	Possible Hedging Instruments
Client likes stocks long term but has short-term concerns about a broad market correction.	Broad market exposure	S&P 500 futures, options, or Depositary Receipts (SPDRs) S&P MidCap 400 futures, options, or SPDRs Russell 2000 futures or options
Client has a concern that technology sector will exhibit seasonal slump but wants to retain long exposure in the event that the sector heats up.	Broad-based sector exposure	Nasdaq-100 futures or options Options on a broad technology sector index Options or futures on a high-technology index
Client has a large position in Lucent Technology but is concerned that weakness among multimedia networking stocks could pull Lucent down.	Specific industry exposure	Options on a multimedia networking index (or other narrow-based sector options, depending on stock to be hedged)
Client has a large position in a very-low-cost-basis stock that is expected to be weak near term.	Company-specific exposure	Single-stock options Sector index options

risk characteristics of the portfolio or stocks being hedged.

Applications of derivatives for risk management include overlay futures hedges to reduce exposures, option-based hedges (puts, put spreads, and collars), and selling index calls to trade upside potential for yield enhancement.

▪ *Selling futures.* Selling futures on the fund's benchmark index is the simplest way to reduce market exposure without liquidating stock positions. Any outperformance of the fund's holdings relative to the benchmark is retained while the futures hedge is in place. The dollar amount of futures sold in relation to the size of the fund can be thought of as equivalent to raising cash—that is, creating a synthetic cash position with a futures position. The return on the synthetic cash is typically the yield of a Eurodollar deposit plus or minus any futures mispricing.

▪ *Hedging with put options.* Index options have long been used by pension funds and institutional money managers for locking in gains on portfolios or reducing downside risk over a short period. In contrast to the futures hedge, hedging with put options allows for some participation in upside moves in the benchmark index. Buying put options reduces downside risk for a range of index levels below a selected strike price. A fund manager who buys an out-of-the-money put option incurs an up-front cost based on the term of the hedge and volatility premium in the option at that time. This up-front cost reduces returns by a fixed amount if the put expires worthless. Puts are favored if the investor is generally bullish but has some concern that a view could be wrong and that equity prices could fall significantly.

▪ *Collars.* Collar strategies combine the purchase of a put with the sale of a call option, thereby limiting the upside participation above the strike of the call sold. Collars are most appropriate if the man-

ager expects a trading-range market with some downside risk.

Investors need to understand the opportunity cost of zero-premium collars in rising market environments before using them. In selecting a hedging strategy, one should not overemphasize the question of what the up-front costs are. Research has shown that going from a fully invested equity position to protecting that position with a zero-premium collar— that is, buying a put/selling a call at an apparent zero cost—can be the beta equivalent of selling as much as half the portfolio's equity exposure. This outcome is fine for an investor who wants it, but some investors that buy zero-premium collars do not understand the magnitude of the effect on overall exposure. So, a collar is a fine strategy if the investor thinks that a trading range is highly likely and that the downside risk is high and the investor wants to significantly reduce equity exposure on the upside in exchange for downside protection.

▪ *Selling call options.* In an option strategy, whether at the stock, the sector, or the index level, an investor who can assign probabilities to the trading range and the upside/downside potential can see where to focus attention. A call-selling strategy can also be a good trading-range strategy for return enhancement and a good strategy for investors who do not expect much downside risk but who want some compensation for limiting their upside potential. In addition to having a desire to enhance returns in a modest-return environment, the investor should assess whether the level of enhancement provided by the options sale is sufficient in light of expected risk or the likelihood of forgoing return in a rising market.

Conclusion

In order to understand the equity derivatives markets, investors should understand the evolution of equity derivatives, realize that products were developed to quickly and efficiently accomplish strategies, and know that index replication is the basic concept that underlies many derivatives. Knowing the important differences that distinguish futures and options and being able to identify conditions that affect the level of derivatives activity help the portfolio manager choose the derivative that best accomplishes the strategy.

Many new derivatives with a wide variety of applications were developed in the 1990s. The strategies that these instruments implement can be divided into four broad categories: to enhance fund management, to achieve asset allocation, to implement view-driven strategies, and to manage risk. Investors should think of derivatives as means to an end, not an end in themselves.

Question and Answer Session

Joanne Hill

Question: When using futures for asset allocation on top of an underlying cash portfolio, how can a fund manager best manage the margin requirements, both initial and variation margin?

Hill: Initial minimum margin is fixed by the exchange (firms may require excess margin) and can be posted in interest-bearing instruments (T-bills). We recommend that, in keeping cash for making the daily variation margin payments, investors watch the volatility of the markets on a daily basis and, to minimize the need to hold excess cash, keep on hand a cash level that reflects a daily move of two to three standard deviations.

Most investors in the United States use "single-currency margining" for international futures. They usually clear (settle) their business with one futures broker (two at most), which makes life a lot simpler than if many brokers were used. The broker does all the margining in local currencies with the exchanges, but the investors can post and receive margin in dollars.

Question: Can derivatives be used to construct a five- to seven-year series of forward prices for an equity portfolio?

Hill: Probably not. That is, you can do anything at a price, but think about what the dealer has to do to quote you that price. Anything from 5 to 10 years will be expensive because the dealer has to consider carrying that position (hedging) and financing it for that amount of time. Typically, equity dealers charge quite a bit for making that kind of a commitment. In addition, the investor bears the credit risk of the dealer to

make good on that commitment over the 5–10 year period. Some insurance companies, however, find long-term commitments to be a more natural fit on their books. Such companies may be involved in forward pricing of equities, which an investor could consider if the investor is comfortable with the credit issues.

Question: If volatility in the equity markets decreases, will volatility in options markets automatically decrease, or will options markets lag?

Hill: We have looked at 1987 and at 1990 around the time of Iraq's invasion of Kuwait to see how long index options take to adapt to lower volatility. They usually take at least 3 months and sometimes as long as 6–12 months. The index option premiums take quite a while to come down, at least 6 months. The result is a wide spread of implied volatility to historical volatility for several months after a high-volatility episode.

Question: Has historical stock market volatility moved greatly from 20 percent?

Hill: Historical stock market volatility depends on what window is examined. For example, historical volatility in October 1997 was more than 30 percent for the month, the most volatile month since 1988. Historical volatility is now in the low 20s. Implied volatility moved up to 35 percent and now is down in the 25 percent range, but the spread is wider. The average spread between implied and historical volatility in indexes, which takes into account the risk of the market maker hedging option

positions, is about 3 percent. In stock options, the spread is closer to zero because the option market maker can diversify among positions and adjust hedges by trading stocks.

Question: Is your calculation of transaction costs in Table 3 for U.S. futures pre or post the S&P futures split? Will this dramatic increase in the cost of using futures reduce institutional use of this market?

Hill: This issue is a controversial topic among dealers and customers. The cost of trading futures has had a long decline over time because the index has gone up. I reduced the cost estimate from 2 bps several years ago to 1 bp, and now it is approximately 1.3 bps. The calculation in Table 3 does not reflect a split in the multiplier. Because the dollar amount is fixed and the index has gone up, the commission costs of using the market have gone down a lot. When stocks split, commissions do not split, so why should everybody be having such a problem with this fact in the futures world?

A lower multiplier is not likely to decrease institutional use of futures. The market has had this cost level before, and it did not impede the growth of the market.

Question: You mentioned that the percentage of stock market capitalization trading every day is about 0.4 percent. Has that percentage been fairly constant in the past 20–25 years?

Hill: It has been fairly constant. The number was 0.48 percent in 1991 and is now 0.43 percent. In Hong Kong and several other markets, the amount of trades per day has also been between 0.4 and 0.5 percent. The ratio for bond trades per day versus bonds outstanding is similar. We all want liquidity, but this ratio is a fact of life for financial assets. With this kind of ratio, the demands on the financial markets can shift a lot in reaction to big news events. Everybody, whether a regulator or an exchange, faces this challenge. The NYSE is installing capacity to trade five times its daily volume for this reason.

Question: How could I try to take advantage of the January effect using derivatives?

Hill: Making a domestic overlay allocation from large cap to small cap is very simple. Perhaps because of the January effect, you would want to tilt away from large S&P 500 stocks into Russell 2000 stocks. You could also do this by selling S&P 500 futures and buying Russell 2000 or S&P MidCap 400 futures. The approach is simple if you shift between the S&P 500 and the Russell 2000: For example, for a $10 million shift, you would simply sell $10 million notional value of S&P 500 futures and buy $10 million in Russell 2000 futures.

Derivatives in Fixed-Income Portfolios

Don M. Chance, CFA
First Union Professor of Financial Risk Management
Virginia Tech

A host of derivative products allows fixed-income portfolio managers to accomplish virtually any strategy. A portfolio manager should select the derivative instrument that best suits the strategy by determining whether the risk to be hedged is broad based or specific, whether the manager is willing to pay a premium for asymmetric return distributions, and whether the manager wants to lock in favorable terms at the outset.

T he use of derivatives in fixed-income portfolios ranges from commonplace exchange-traded futures and options to custom-tailored four-party credit swaps. This presentation first provides a broad survey of products and strategies and then focuses on several less-well-known products—interest rate swaptions and credit derivatives. Credit derivatives are the newest life form on the derivatives horizon.[1]

Bond derivatives, interest rate derivatives, and so forth, are often discussed as if they were the same, but there is a key distinction between derivatives on bonds and derivatives on interest rates. Derivatives on bonds are instruments that pay off based on movements in the prices of the underlying bonds themselves. These derivatives consist of futures and options on bonds, options on futures, forward contracts on bonds, options on forward contracts on bonds, and structured notes and asset-backed securities. Callable bonds are also derivatives on bonds. For interest rate derivatives, the payoff is based on movements in the underlying interest rate. Such derivatives are forward rate agreements, interest rate swaps, options on interest rates, options on swaps (swaptions), and options on forward rate agreements. Interest rates and bond prices are tied together, of course, by what happens to the term structure and the credit risk structure.

The Markets

The designated exchanges are the heart of the futures and options industry. On the exchanges, one can find futures, options on futures, and options on bonds.

The bigger market for fixed-income derivatives, however, is the OTC or dealer market, where swaps, options, forward rate agreements, forward contracts and options on bonds, structured notes, and asset-backed securities trade. The major differences between the two markets are as follows:

- *Standardization.* The exchange provides standardized deals; the OTC market provides customized deals.
- *Credit risk.* Trading on the exchanges entails no credit risk because the exchange acts as a clearinghouse for all trades; OTC trading involves credit risk.
- *Transparency.* Trades on the futures exchanges are transparent. Transactions are reported; they come across the screen; and people often know who is doing what. In the OTC market, transactions are private. The two counterparties fill out the paperwork, and the rest of the world does not know what they did. They may end up reporting what they did at some time, but the market is relatively private.
- *Liquidity.* The exchanges maintain that they have the more liquid markets, and some of them are; the Eurodollar market and S&P 500 Index futures markets, for example, are incredibly liquid. Others, however, are not liquid. The catastrophe insurance pits at the Chicago Board of Trade were a fantastic idea, but the market has not fully developed. So, although it probably will be liquid some day, it is not right now.

---

[1]For further reading on derivatives, see Keith C. Brown, ed., *Derivative Strategies for Managing Portfolio Risk* (Charlottesville, VA: AIMR, 1993); Keith C. Brown and D. J. Smith, *Interest Rate and Currency Swaps: A Tutorial* (Charlottesville, VA: AIMR, 1995); Gary Gastineau and Mark P. Kritzman, *The Dictionary of Financial Risk Management* [book online], revised ed. (http://www.amex.com/findic, 1997).

The OTC market varies in terms of liquidity. OTC instruments are not designed for someone to buy one day and then sell a couple of days later. Investors can make the attempt—enter the market offering the opposite transaction—but the other side of the deal may not offset the first transaction. If an investor opens and closes a futures contract, the result is a washout, and if an investor opens a swap and offsets the swap with an identical swap, it washes out. But if an investor simply takes the opposite position in the OTC market, he or she will probably have a different counterparty and both swaps will remain on the investor's books, so the credit risk still exists. In that sense, the OTC markets are less liquid than the futures markets.

- *Costs.* Although the deals are customized in the OTC markets, the markets are not necessarily more expensive than the exchanges in terms of transaction costs. For plain-vanilla instruments, the OTC market is a fairly liquid, low-cost market.

Fixed-income derivative markets are tied to the fixed-income money and capital markets through the term structure of interest rates and the credit risk structure of interest rates, as shown in **Figure 1**. To some people, the term structure is the wonderful thing about fixed-income securities; to others, it is what makes fixed-income investing so complicated. The equity markets have no such arbitrage relationship that relates one stock to another stock by some formula, but if credit risk is stripped away, such relationships do exist among all the fixed-income instruments. If the market is considered to be U.S. Treasury securities alone, for example, the instruments are clearly related to each other. In fact, some institutions will take any two of the instruments and create a third one, which determines the prices investors pay.

On the other side of the picture is the link through the credit risk structure of interest rates. The

credit risk structure begins with separating credit risk into categories—low, medium, and high or, going further, as the rating agencies do, Aaa, Aa, A, and so forth. Then, the credit risk structure asks how much additional return a party expects to receive based on the additional credit risk the party assumed under the rating structure.

The term structure is easier to understand and to "price" (to determine how much additional return one should receive for the maturity) than credit risk.

Interest Rate Derivatives

All interest rate derivatives share the following characteristics:

- *Notional principal.* All have a notional principal, the amount used to determine the specific interest payment.
- *Payoff basis.* The payoff is based on the difference between one rate—the contract rate—and the floating rate. Normally, the parties exchange only the net difference to minimize credit risk or counterparty risk.
- *Counterparty risk.* The risk is low because the amount at risk is only the net of two interest payments—one going one way and the other going the other way at the same time.
- *Complexity.* In terms of simplicity versus complexity of pricing, futures, forwards, and swaps fall into the simple category and options fall into the complex category.

Understanding the characteristics and variations of specific interest rate derivatives—forward rate agreements, interest rate options, swaps and swaptions, and interest rate futures—facilitates deciding which derivative will be the most appropriate for a particular application or will achieve the intended strategy.

Forward Rate Agreements. A forward rate agreement (FRA) is a contract between two parties that has a specific maturity date and calls for a single interest payment to be made by one party at a fixed rate with the opposite party paying a floating or variable rate that will be determined at a future date. It involves one specific payment and is basically a one-date swap (in the sense that a swap is a combination of FRAs with some variations). As for settlement, the FRA expires on one date and settles at that time or within two business days. Each counterparty assumes the risk that the other will default.

An investor takes a long position in anticipation of rising interest rates. The investor goes long the underlying rate, which is usually LIBOR, essentially the Eurodollar rate. The investor who goes long LIBOR pays the dealer a fixed interest payment,

Figure 1. How Fixed-Income Derivatives Tie in with the Fixed-Income Markets

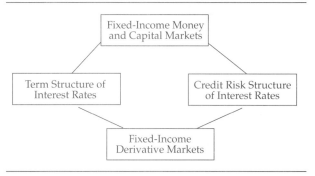

which is a known payment on a given date, and the dealer pays the investor whatever LIBOR turns out to be on the expiration date.

The pricing—that is, how the investor knows what the appropriate fixed rate is—is fairly simple. Basically, it is the forward rate, so all the investor needs to know is the term structure of interest rates.

Interest Rate Options. An interest rate option is a contract that gives the investor the right to make a known fixed interest rate payment in exchange for receiving a future unknown or floating interest rate payment. An interest rate call option gives the holder the right to make a fixed-rate payment and receive a floating-rate payment. A put option gives the right to receive fixed and pay floating.

Interest rate options have a notional principal amount (similar to the Chicago Board Options Exchange [CBOE] requirement that one option equal an option on 100 shares of stock). The notional principal might be $5 million, $10 million, $20 million, or so on. For instance, the option might be described as "an option on the interest payments on $20 million."

The payout is typically deferred until after the option's expiration. This characteristic, which is also found with swaps, differentiates the interest rate option from the FRA. Typically, the actual payment occurs 90 or 180 days after expiration (although it could be structured differently) because interest rate options are generally used to hedge interest rate risk on a floating-rate loan that the investor has taken out as a borrower or a lender. In a floating-rate loan, the interest rate is normally reset twice a year; then, interest accrues at that rate and the interest payment is made at the end of the period. So, the rate is set at the beginning and the interest is paid at the end. Most people do not like surprises; they want to know right at the outset what the interest rate is and what payment they will make on the interest payment date.

When the investor's option expires, it is either in the money or out of the money. For the call to expire in the money, the interest rate has to rise above the strike rate, and for a put to end up in the money, the rate has to drop below the strike rate. The option can be a European option, which can be exercised only at expiration, or an American option, which can be exercised at or any time prior to expiration.

As in any option, the writer bears no default risk, because the buyer does not have to do anything. The buyer puts money on the table and then has the right, but no obligation, to do something later. In contrast to the options at the CBOE or the options on futures at the Chicago Mercantile Exchange, where the exchange guarantees the payment, the buyer of an interest rate option faces the risk of the writer defaulting.

The pricing of interest rate options is complex.

The only way to do it is to build a complete model of the term structure.[2] An analyst who knows something about binomial (decision tree) models can quickly pick up the basics of term-structure modeling.

■ *Caps.* Some people would equate caps with interest rate options. A cap is typically a series, portfolio, or combination of independent interest rate call options that expire on different dates. The buyer of a cap is usually a borrower or issuer of a floating-rate note who wants to hedge against higher interest rates. For example, the cap buyer may have issued a one-year floating-rate note requiring quarterly interest payments for the next year. The issuer is thus exposed to the interest rate increasing every quarter. So, the issuer buys a series of call options timed to expire on each of the quarterly reset dates of the floating-rate note. If rates increase, the call option expires in the money and compensates the buyer for the difference between the rate and the strike rate that the buyer chose for the call option. The buyer receives this payment three months later, which coincides with the interest payment date on the floating-rate note.

This series of caps is termed "independent" because exercising one of them does not affect the buyer's ability to exercise the next one. An interest rate option can be structured so that the options are in some way dependent on each other, an arrangement called a compound option.

A borrower that buys an independent series of caps benefits from falling rates and does not get hurt above the strike price by rising rates. The buyer does have to pay cash up front for the options, so if the buyer sets the strike at, say, 10 percent, the cost will actually be a little more than 10 percent because of the cap premium.

■ *Floors.* Interest rate floors protect lenders or holders of floating-rate notes or bonds against falling rates. A floor is a series of independent put options set up in such a way that on the reset date, if the rate falls below the strike rate level, the put option is in the money. The buyer of the put option then exercises it and, at the next payment date on the note, receives a cash payment that compensates for the decline in the interest rate on the floating-rate note. Again, the buyer must obviously pay cash up front for the floor.

■ *Collars.* Putting a cap and a floor together creates a collar. It is often called a "zero-cost collar," but in reality, nothing has zero cost. In a collar, a borrower will buy a cap to protect against rising rates

[2]See David Heath, Robert Jarrow, and Andrew Morton, "Bond Pricing and the Term Structure of Interest Rates: A New Methodology," *Econometrica*, vol. 60, no. 1 (1992):77–106, and Thomas S.Y. Ho and Sang Bin Lee, "Term Structure Movements and Pricing Interest Rate Contingent Claims," *Journal of Finance*, vol. 41, no.5 (1986):1011–30.

on the floating-rate reset dates and sell a floor to a party on the other side of the contract (who will benefit if rates fall below the strike price). The cap and the floor have different exercise prices. For example, suppose an investor who buys a cap and sells a floor sets the cap strike rate at 11 percent and the floor strike rate at 9 percent. The interest rate is then capped on the upside at 11 percent and floored on the downside at 9 percent. A lender would do the opposite collar—buy a floor and sell a cap.

The premium on the cap and the premium on the floor need not fully offset; they may be wholly or only partially offsetting. But the term "zero-cost collar" comes from the idea of offsetting premiums.

To pick the cap and floor strike prices, the investor needs a way of pricing the options. A floating-rate borrower who decides to buy a cap may wonder about ways to reduce the cost of the cap. A derivatives dealer will tell the borrower, "You can reduce the cost if you sell me a floor." The 11 percent cap limits upside interest rate risk at 11 percent, and the dealer wants the borrower to sell him a floor at 9 percent because the dealer has figured out that the price of the call options with an 11 percent exercise rate exactly equals the price of the put options with a 9 percent exercise rate. (Of course, these numbers are simply examples; actual strike rates depend on the implied volatility and other terms of the contract.) Although buying a cap struck at 11 percent and selling a floor struck at 9 percent does not require payment of a premium (hence, the term "zero-premium collar"), it does cost something. The dealer will say it does not cost anything, but what it does cost is anything the borrower would have saved if interest rates fell below 9 percent. So, although the investor does not put cash down on the table, the investor definitely gives up something. The cost is similar to the cost of a covered call: If an investor owns a stock and then sells a call option on that stock, the investor receives the option premium but forgoes all of a bull market if it occurs.

The collar is a popular strategy not only in fixed-income investing but also in equity investing.

Interest Rate Swaps. This instrument is extremely popular, perhaps because it came into the market faster than other derivatives. The interest rate swap is a fairly simple instrument in comparison with options, especially in terms of pricing—that is, establishing what the fixed rate should be.

The interest rate swap is a contract in which two parties agree to exchange a series of future interest payments. In the plain-vanilla swap, one party makes payments at one rate that is known (a fixed rate) and the other makes payments at a future rate that is unknown or at a floating rate, typically set to LIBOR.

Obviously, the investor could be on either side of the transaction.

The interest rate swap market is the biggest of the swap markets, and the plain-vanilla swap is the most prevalent structure within that market. Although the size of the swap market in notional terms is about $20 trillion today, the market is actually nowhere near that big in terms of net interest payments on the notional principal.

The net payment is determined on a certain date based on a certain rate but generally deferred until the end of the settlement period—usually three months or six months later. The payment does not have to be structured that way, however; arrears swaps settle up and pay at the same time, within a two-business-day settlement period.

Each party assumes the risk of the other defaulting, but because the parties exchange only the net payment, the risk from one party defaulting is reduced.

The pricing of interest rate swaps, based only on the term structure, is simple. Hedging can be done by buying and selling bonds or other derivatives.

All sorts of swaps are possible—equity swaps (swapping an equity payment for another equity payment or something else, such as an interest payment), commodity swaps (involving oil or gold, for example). A popular variation is the currency swap, in which one party pays in one currency and the other party pays in another currency. Variants of the currency swap are possible: One party could pay fixed, the other floating; both could pay floating; both could pay fixed.

A basis swap, in which both rates are unknown, is a variation of the interest rate swap. A typical basis swap requires one party to pay LIBOR and the other, the dealer, to pay the U.S. T-bill rate. This variation is called the TED (Treasury–Eurodollar) spread swap.

Constant-maturity swaps or yield-curve swaps are a form of basis swap. These swaps allow each counterparty to participate in changes in the shape of the yield curve. For example, in exchange for paying LIBOR, one counterparty will receive the yield on the 10-year constant maturity T-bond (possibly less a predetermined spread) that is prevailing on each reset date. Thus, the party paying LIBOR benefits when the yield curve steepens or when short rates decrease and long rates increase.

Another variation is the index amortizing (or, on the other side, accreting) swap, which is designed to reduce prepayment risk by having the notional principal change with the level of market interest rates. If interest rates decrease, mortgage portfolio managers know they will experience more prepayments on their mortgage portfolios. An index amortizing swap has a schedule that indicates how the notional principal adjusts downward when interest rates decrease, so the interest payments on that notional principal decrease. This swap does not perfectly hedge prepayment risk (it hedges prepayment risk associated with interest rates, not prepayment risk associated with demographics), but it at least moves the notional principal on the swap in the general direction that the principal on the mortgage portfolio is moving.

Differential swaps, "diff swaps," involve the exchange of cash flows based on short-term interest rates in two different countries but denominated in the same currency. This type of swap allows a fixed-income portfolio manager to take advantage of relative changes in the shape of the yield curve between two countries without having to directly hold nondomestic securities.

Interest Rate Swaptions. Interest rate swaptions, which are options on interest rate swaps, can be very confusing at first. The starting point for understanding them is to understand a swap—the contract for a series of interest payments with one side paying a fixed rate and the other side paying a floating rate. The swaption is an option that provides the right to enter a swap as a fixed-rate payer or a fixed-rate receiver, with the fixed rate established in advance. As in any option, the investor picks the desired strike price and buys the right to enter into a swap at a fixed rate. The investor chooses to be a fixed-rate payer or a fixed-rate receiver. Those two choices are called, respectively, "payer swaptions" and "receiver swaptions." The setup is no different from someone saying, "I want to buy a call option (or I want to buy a put option), and I will choose the exercise rate." The terms "call" and "put" are not used much in connection with swaptions, but the concept is the same.

A swaption has a notional principal that is, as in all derivatives, a big number—$5 million, $10 million, $20 million—based on the amount of exposure the investor has. That notional principal on the swaption corresponds to the notional principal on the related swap. For example, suppose you are thinking you might need an option on a swap. You define it as $10 million, $5 million, or whatever and seek an option to enter into a specific swap.

The swaption itself expires on a given day, specified as American or European style. The underlying swap has its own credit risk. The buyer of the swaption accepts the risk of the writer defaulting. That is, the buyer of the option to enter into the swap risks the possibility that when the time comes to exercise it, the counterparty will have gone bankrupt and not be able to enter into the swap. The seller or writer accepts having to enter into a swap at a below-market

rate (as the fixed-rate receiver) for a payer swaption or having to enter into a swap at an above-market rate (as the fixed-rate payer) for a receiver swaption.

At the expiration date, how the swaption is exercised depends on what the two parties decided when they wrote the contract. Exercise can be by cash settlement or by establishing the underlying swap. For example, if I have a swaption on a three-year swap with a rate of 9 percent, when the swaption expires, if the swaption is in the money and I exercise it, I enter into a three-year swap with a fixed rate of 9 percent. Later, I can go into the market and offset that rate or enter into the opposite transaction. The process is similar to buying a call at the CBOE and, when the time comes to exercise it, acquiring XYZ stock: I can hold on to the stock, or I can sell it. In this case, I can hold on to the swap—it is in the money, so it is worth something—or I can enter into the opposite transaction to, in effect, liquidate it.

Cash settlement means that the two parties agree on a method of pricing the underlying swap. When the swaption expires, the parties figure out that it is in the money by a certain amount and one party simply pays the other. If the contract is worth $500,000, then the writer pays the buyer that amount. This form of exercise is standard for S&P 500 Index options.

A swap rate is basically a par bond rate. Pricing is complicated and requires a model of the evolution of the term structure. Although fixed-rate swap prices are quoted off the Treasury yield curve, they are priced off the relevant forward curve. For example, a pay fixed/receive LIBOR swap would be priced off the LIBOR forward curve. The pay-fixed rate would be established by equating the present value of the fixed cash flows to the present value of the cash flows implied by the LIBOR forward rates.

Swaptions are bets on movements in swap rates, which are only one kind of interest rate.

▪ *The payer swaption.* A payer swaption is the right to enter a swap as a fixed-rate payer/floating-rate receiver. The payer always specifies what the underlying floating rate is—LIBOR, the Eurodollar rate, or so on. The instrument is similar to an interest rate call option. Payer swaptions are used when interest rates are expected to increase. If interest rates move up (if the term structure shifts up), the swap rate goes up with it. So, the security that provides the right to pay a lower rate as interest rates rise is a valuable instrument. For example, suppose the instrument is a three-year payer swaption—that is, the option itself expires in three years—and you, as the payer, have the right to pay fixed and receive floating on a four-year swap with an exercise rate of 9 percent. That is, in three years, you have the right to enter into a four-year pay-fixed swap at 9 percent.

Suppose you decide to use LIBOR as the floating rate. Now, on the expiration date, if the rate on four-year swaps is more than 9 percent, you will exercise that swaption (assuming it is a European option or you did not exercise it earlier). The value at expiration is the present value of a four-year annuity equal to the difference between the market rate and the strike rate of 9 percent.

The small transaction cost, the bid–ask spread and so on, slightly changes the price. For example, suppose the pay-fixed rate on current four-year swaps is 10 percent on the expiration date of the payer swaption. Thus, the payer swaption with a 9 percent strike rate is in the money by 1 percent. Exercising the payer swaption and simultaneously entering into an offsetting four-year swap as the fixed-rate receiver results in a four-year annuity of 1 percent, probably semiannually, on the notional principal amount. It does not matter at all what the floating rate is because the floating payment and the floating receipt offset.

Swaptions basically create annuities. What is that annuity worth? You can figure out the present value of a four-year annuity of 1 percent if you know what the term structure is. Counterparties can agree to calculate the value of the annuity and agree at the outset that the writer will pay the buyer the value of the annuity if the swaption is in the money, and if it is out of the money, the buyer receives nothing and the swaption expires worthless.

▪ *Receiver swaptions.* The receiver swaption is the right to enter as a fixed-rate receiver/floating-rate payer. The receiver swaption is the opposite of the payer swaption and increases in value when interest rates decline. A receiver swaption is the right to receive the strike rate, so it is like an interest rate put option. The payer swaption is somewhat like an interest rate call option (it does not create the same outcome as an interest rate call option, but it does profit in the same kind of market), and the opposite is true for receiver swaptions.

The way swaptions work illustrates the importance of focusing on these derivatives as interest rate derivatives rather than bond derivatives. A market in which a payer swaption will be valuable is not the market in which a bond will be valuable. Bond markets are bearish when interest rates increase; bonds are not attractive then, but payer swaptions and call options are. Interest rate derivatives and bond derivatives are related. For bond derivatives, however, investors need to think about prices; for interest rate derivatives, they need to think about interest rates.

Interest Rate Futures. Interest rate futures trade on the futures exchanges in standardized contracts in which two parties agree to buy or sell a fixed-income security or, sometimes, a future interest payment at an agreed price. Profits/losses on these contracts are settled and distributed every day. They are subject to the rules and regulations of the exchanges on which they trade and, in the United States, to a federal regulatory agency, the Commodity Futures Trading Commission.

The two main types of interest rate futures are T-bond futures and Eurodollar futures, which are the primary short-term interest rate futures instruments. Although T-bond futures have been in existence longer, Eurodollar futures have significantly higher trading volume. Eurodollar futures contracts are widely used by swap market makers to hedge their books. In fact, the success of the Eurodollar futures contract parallels the success and growth of the OTC swap market.

Interest rate futures have standard delivery terms, expiration dates, and contract sizes. Eurodollar futures have a standard $1 million face value and standard final trading and settlement date, namely, the second London business day before the third Wednesday of the delivery month (March, June, September, and December). Generally, the terms cannot be changed, but the futures exchanges have occasionally allowed some flexibility in the terms.

A major distinction between these instruments and the OTC instruments is that parties in a futures contract incur no default risk—that is, assuming the futures exchange does not default through its clearinghouse. A clearinghouse going under would be a very bad sign indeed for the economy. It has never happened.

For T-bonds, physical delivery is made; it is made by wire, but the specific underlying bond does have to be transferred. For Eurodollar futures, settlement is in cash for the net cash value of making delivery.

The pricing of interest rate futures is fairly simple. Pricing is based on the net of the opportunity cost of carry over the yield. As in a T-bond yielding a coupon and having a carrying cost, the process boils down to figuring out the difference between the coupon and the carrying cost and adding or subtracting it, whichever way the difference is, to the cash or spot market price of the instrument.

Applications of Fixed-Income Derivatives

Almost all of the instruments described so far can be used in any of the following situations. Some are better than others, and one instrument may require a little more sophistication in the trading than another, but almost all of them will work. Sometimes, an investor will choose a particular instrument on a given day not because of the payoff or because extra cash needs to be invested but because, for some reason, the price is better on that instrument on that day. The price differential could be the result of a temporary arbitrage opportunity in the market.

Applications. One application is to lock in the purchase or sale price of a fixed-income security or portfolio. If an investor anticipates buying a security or selling a security already owned, using any of these derivatives can help lock in the price. For example, suppose I am going to buy a bond. If I buy a call option on the bond, I then have the right to buy that bond at a fixed price.

Derivatives can also be used to adjust a portfolio's market exposure, duration, or convexity. Whether the manager practices delta hedging (hedging the first-order risk) or gamma hedging (hedging the second-order risk) or hedging duration and convexity, the manager can adjust that duration using derivatives. Derivatives can quickly and efficiently increase or decrease market exposure. The manager could change exposure by buying and selling the underlying bonds, but derivatives are a lot cheaper to buy and sell in terms of transaction costs. In addition, they offer ways of generating payouts and profits that are unavailable to portfolio managers restricted to direct buying and selling of bonds.

Hedging cash inflows and outflows is a third application. These flows can be a major problem for managers, who may have to reduce their portfolios by huge amounts or absorb huge inflows that, at least briefly, change the portfolio's market exposure. A manager can easily use derivatives during that time to maintain the desired market exposure.

Fixed-income derivatives can also increase the rate of return on lending at the expense of accepting counterparty credit risk. If you buy a bond and it has a certain yield, you can often enhance that yield by entering into a swap. For example, by entering into a swap to convert, say, a fixed rate to a floating rate or a floating rate to a fixed rate, a firm can get a comparatively better rate than if the firm had issued that type of instrument in the first place. The quality spread differential—between a AAA-rated issuer and a BBB-rated issuer, for example—creates an apparent opportunity for credit risk arbitrage based on the principle of comparative advantage. The key decision involves evaluating the marginal increase in yield in exchange for an acceptable level of credit risk. This is the same approach one would apply to compare an A-rated bond with a BBB-rated bond: How much more yield can I get for the added credit risk? Is the return worth the additional risk?

Finally, fixed-income derivatives allow one to convert a floating-rate security to a fixed-rate security. For example, a company that is currently borrowing at a floating rate and is worried about rates going up can easily switch to a fixed rate by entering into a pay fixed/receive floating swap. The floating rate on the swap and the floating rate on the corporate bond will offset, and the company will end up paying a fixed rate, with possibly a built-in spread.

Matching Derivative to Application. Deciding which type of fixed-income derivative is the most appropriate for a particular application involves three issues.

The first issue is whether the risk to be hedged is generic and broad based or more specific to a security or portfolio. If the risk is generic or broad based—for example, if the underlying factor driving the portfolio is exposure to long-term T-bonds—then T-bond futures contracts or options on futures will be good instruments to use. If you have a specific portfolio of securities and you do not think its risk can be properly reflected in a broad market instrument (such as the long-term T-bond futures contract), then you probably need a more customized instrument. You might go to a dealer and say, "Here is my exposure in this portfolio. Give me an instrument that will pay off based on this exposure." That approach will be a little more expensive than using a standard derivative.

The second issue is: Are you willing to pay cash up front for the flexibility of being able to profit from movements in the right direction and not lose by movements in the wrong direction? If so, then options are the appropriate vehicle.

Third, if you anticipate the possibility of needing a swap at a future date and you want to lock in favorable terms right now, then a swaption is your best instrument.

Credit Derivatives

A credit derivative is a contract or transaction designed to separate the risk of default from the risk of movements in the underlying market. A credit derivative can be traded separately to hedge or speculate on credit risk. Credit derivatives are literally a market for credit alone.

The credit derivatives market is evolving, and much needs to be learned about it. A lot of institutions deal in this business, but they are still sorting out what they are doing. The tasks of understanding, pricing, and trading credit risk are difficult.

The first level of credit risk analysis is what a typical small town bank does in deciding whether to make a loan to a local business: The bank asks that the company submit financial statements (probably every quarter) and looks over those statements; the bank president plays golf with the president of the company and gets a feel for whether the person is honest; the president has been doing business with the applicant for years and feels good about the loan. So, the bank extends the credit. This first level is a fairly crude credit analysis. The process has evolved, however, into credit scoring models; the bankers plug in the financial numbers, the model comes up with a score, and they compare that score with some standard to decide whether to lend.

Another level of credit risk analysis is to look at the Moody's Investors Service and Standard & Poor's Corporation ratings, in the belief that what they do is pretty sophisticated.

The derivatives business has become concerned about the credit issue in the past several years, even though the credit risk on derivatives is only a small fraction of the credit risk on loans. On a $1 million loan, $1 million must be paid back, whereas on a notional principal of $1 million in a swap, probably only 1–3 percent of that money is at risk. When that risk is translated into the $20 trillion market, however, it is big enough to cause concern.

Professionals in the derivatives industry, who have developed some fairly sophisticated models, have now turned their attention to modeling credit risk. There is an underlying way of modeling credit risk as an option, but it works only for the simplest loan one could create—such as a zero-coupon bond—and it works only for companies that have simple capital structures. So, figuring out how much credit risk is in a fixed-income security and what premium should be charged is complex. Nevertheless, derivatives on credit risk—options, futures, and swaps—are being written.

If one party gets rid of the credit risk by using a credit derivative, someone else obviously has to take it. The credit derivative allows the low-cost acceptance of market risk (interest rate risk, currency risk, and so forth) and avoidance of credit risk—or vice versa.

Credit derivatives will improve loan pricing as fixed-income markets, derivatives markets, and loan markets become more integrated. Most large banks have a commercial lending operation that is separate from its derivatives operation. The two functions use different methods, and the derivatives side generally uses the latest technology and is more sophisticated than the lending side. If they are not properly pricing credit the same way, however, they are not pricing credit risk. If the bank is doing a good job, it will eventually integrate its risk-management systems so that the people pricing loans and the people pricing derivatives come together. Top management will realize that derivatives can be used to reduce or increase exposure to market risk and credit risk. This coordination will make the loan market a lot more competitive than it is, which will benefit borrowers.

Types. The most common type of credit derivative is a "total-return swap." Other types are credit options, credit swaps, and credit-linked securities.

■ *Total-return swaps.* This swap is not an innovation connected with credit derivatives; it has existed for a while, but only recently was it identified as a kind of credit derivative. In the total-return swap, one party pays the other the total return on an underlying asset. For example, suppose the underlying asset were a bond (it could be a loan), one party would pay the other the total return on that bond, and the other would pay a floating rate (or any agreed-upon rate).

The total return is the interest and any capital appreciation, or depreciation, that results from movements in the market interest rates or changes in credit spreads. The floating rate reflects movements in market interest rates. **Figure 2** illustrates the sequence of cash flows for a total-return swap on an underlying Baa-rated corporate note (it could have any rating, although a swap on a Aaa-rated note would not make much sense). On one side is the

Figure 2. Example of a Total-Return Swap

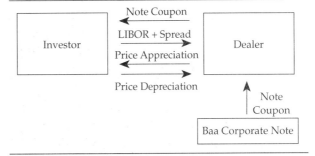

dealer, or any party, that holds the bond and receives the coupon. If the dealer does not want to sell that bond, it can strip the credit risk off so that the dealer pays the coupon and any price appreciation and gets back, say, LIBOR plus a spread—positive, negative, or zero, depending on how the credit risk is priced. The dealer now receives LIBOR, so the dealer now has the interest rate risk. The investor or counterparty will now bear the default risk of the underlying corporate note or event risk that may widen the yield spread.

The total-return swap is not a perfect stripping of market risk from credit risk, but it works fairly well. It is a simple transaction that has been around since before credit derivatives existed, and it is similar to an equity swap.

■ *Credit options and credit swaps.* A credit option or swap is a derivative in which one party's payments are contingent on the occurrence of a credit event (that is, something that affects credit spreads). The two parties have to agree that a credit event has occurred. A Chapter 11 filing or missing an interest payment is a credit event. A rating downgrade or upgrade is a credit event if the two parties decided to define it that way at the start; a restructuring might also be a credit event. One party pays a premium and buys an option that pays off in the event of a credit event. Deciding how much it pays off in which events can be difficult. The option will contain a formula that states what the payoff is to the option holder.

A simple variation of the credit option is an option on the credit spread. The credit spread, or yield spread over Treasuries of the same maturity, varies, so one could create an option or forward contract on a credit spread. If that spread widens, credit risk increases and the option begins to move into the money. The payoff formula might state that if the credit spread is 400 basis points (with a strike price of 300 bps), the option is in the money by 100 bps, and the formula will multiply that amount by some percentage for the payoff.

A credit option requires a third party, a dealer that is willing to write the option and guarantee it. An interesting aspect to such a derivative is that one party enters into a transaction to reduce the credit risk of a third party but assumes the credit risk of the counterparty to the transaction. Depending on whether the transaction is an option or a swap, the counterparty could assume some credit risk from the first party. This complication points out how complex credit derivatives can be.

Credit swaps involve one party making a series of fixed payments while the other party makes its payments only when the credit event occurs. A credit swap is more like an option than a swap in that way.

In one variation, four parties are involved. The first party pays the second if a third has a credit event, and the second pays the first if a fourth has a credit event. In addition, the first and the second assume credit risk from each other.

■ *Credit-linked securities.* This instrument is a fixed-income derivative in which the interest payment or principal payment is linked to the credit of a third party. That is, the interest or principal payments can pay off based on whether the third party experiences a credit event.

Some Considerations. First, the market for credit derivatives is not yet very liquid, and it may never be. A lot of transactions occur, but the transactions are based on the credit of a single counterparty,

not generic, marketwide credit risk. Credit options and swaps will probably someday be based on standard market measures. For example, one or more of the rating services will establish average rates on the various ratings, and derivatives will be based on those averages.

The pricing of credit derivatives is much more complex and controversial than the pricing of transactions carrying market risk. Therefore, a lot of discussion about pricing will continue.

Another important consideration for banks is the effect of these instruments on their capital requirements. This issue is also the subject of considerable discussion, particularly by the regulators, and the outcome is not clear.

Other concerns relate to how credit risk is managed and how credit and market risk are related. No one can simply decide to strip off and sell all credit risk. Clearly, if one party lays off credit risk, someone else has to accept it. For example, perhaps a bank has made so many loans to one party that it is uncomfortable with the risk but wants to make another loan to that same party. To do so, the bank can strip off the credit risk and sell it to someone else. Another bank or a dealer might be perfectly willing to accept that credit risk. The market knows how to strip off this risk, but a liquid market has not yet developed.

Credit derivatives are the hottest new family of products, however, and they bring a whole new dimension to buying and selling risk. Credit risk is probably the oldest kind of financial risk, and these derivatives give the industry a handle on how to buy it and sell it.

Conclusion

Derivative products have brought significant innovation to the fixed-income market. Portfolio managers can use interest rate options, interest rate and currency swaps, futures, and swaptions to enhance performance and control risk.

These instruments allow portfolio managers to lock in the purchase or selling price of a debt security, hedge interest rate or credit risk, hedge anticipated cash inflows and outflows, modify a portfolio's duration, and take advantage of arbitrage opportunities. Investors should carefully select the derivative product for the particular application to accomplish the desired strategy.

The new class of products called "credit derivatives" allows investors to separate market risk from credit risk, which provides investors the opportunity to detach and trade the credit risk—either hedging it or accepting more of it.

Question and Answer Session

Don M. Chance, CFA

Question: What are the primary factors that influence swap spreads?

Chance: You might think the swap spread (the spread over the rate for a Treasury security of the same maturity) would be influenced primarily by the credit risk, but the swap market is one of those markets—participants are AA-rated or better—where you either qualify to do swaps or you don't. So, a certain minimum level of credit risk is built in; the market doesn't give one person one rate and someone with better credit a better rate. What really goes into the swap spread is the cost that the dealer incurs in running the hedge book and in managing the dealer's risk. Transaction costs, and so forth, enter the picture, but the dealer also has to think about such aspects as how easy it will be to lay off that swap. For an exotic swap, the spread will be very high; for a plain-vanilla swap, it will be fairly low—probably between 5 and 10 bps.

Question: Please comment on the effectiveness of value-at-risk (VAR) analysis to manage the inherent risk in fixed-income derivatives.

Chance: No topic in my lifetime in this business has been so controversial as VAR. The concept is simple: How much money do you have at risk (the 1 percent or the 5 percent tail) or how much could you lose over a certain period with a certain probability? It is controversial for a couple of reasons. One is that VAR can be calculated in a lot of ways, and some interesting studies have pointed out how divergent those values can be. Also, a lot of people are worried about the subjective element—market experience and

personal judgment. For example, if a regulator tells the banks they can use VAR to meet the requirements for risk management, the regulator has to feel very confident that the banks will produce good estimates and that they understand VAR. The banks must also feel confident that regulators are not simply going to look at that number and say it's acceptable or not.

VAR can't replace the experience and judgment that is built up through years and years of dealing with these markets. VAR is a good little tool in your toolbox (it is a dollar number you can understand, and it will probably be more understandable to your CEO than standard deviations), but you can't rely on it too much. It is also an evolving tool, and I think the controversy will not die out soon.

Question: Please comment on the creation of a forward curve for credit spreads for credit derivatives.

Chance: I suspect it is being done, but I haven't heard much about it. For a plain-vanilla swap, 10 Wall Street firms would price it very similarly. When the credit spread is turned into an option, the prices will vary because each firm will plug in a different level of volatility. The credit derivatives market is similar; it is still in the development stage, and pricing is unclear and controversial. I think firms have forward curves, but I expect they vary considerably.

Question: Wouldn't pricing credit spreads based on credit ratings be a lot easier than pricing single spreads for individual firms?

Chance: Using the credit-rating agencies' ratings would be some-

what like second-generation pricing, in that they draw the line to define Aaa, Aa, and so on. The Wall Street firms don't necessarily look at credit risk that way. They are working on their own models that measure risk in terms of how much VAR a bond will introduce—marginal VAR or delta VAR. J.P. Morgan's CreditMetrics, for example, will give you a sense of the way the market is moving in terms of credit risk.

Question: What steps should an organization take to reduce market risk and the continued losses of fixed-income derivative positions gone bad?

Chance: The answer depends somewhat on what positions they already have in place. The most important thing to understand is that, like it or not, you are risk takers, and like it or not, you have a VAR whether you know it or not. You have exposure—market risk and probably credit risk. So, you must have a risk-management system. You need independent oversight to see if the transactions are being done properly.

If you want to reduce the market risk of a bond portfolio, you can go through your broker or you can sell futures on a T-bond. In this way, you definitely reduce market risk. But what happens if the person who sells those futures contracts enters a 4,000 instead of a 400? What happens if (and it does happen), in an attempt to dig a way out of a hole, someone doubles the bet? The most important risk-management tool is someone with independent oversight making sure that while you are trying to reduce risk, you aren't actually increasing it. The line between hedging and speculation is thin.

Derivatives for International Investing

Thomas S.Y. Ho
Executive Vice President
BARRA, Incorporated

A variety of derivative instruments—ranging from generic cross-currency swaps to basket swaptions—help investors and portfolio managers manage fixed-income and equity exposure in global portfolios. Understanding the risk of each instrument is important, but including derivatives in a portfolio requires analyzing exposure in terms of overall portfolio risk. Several analytical tools, including key-rate duration and value-at-risk analysis, can help analysts identify each source of risk and effectively manage risk at the portfolio level.

Derivatives offer investors a variety of ways to create exposure to and manage the risks in global fixed-income, equity, and currency markets. Since the development of the swap market started in 1981, the types and complexity of derivative instruments with international applications have significantly increased. Derivatives that create or manage exposure to various markets now range from plain-vanilla currency swaps to such complex swaps as basket swaptions and rainbow swaps with embedded cancel swaptions.

This presentation identifies the currency swaps that investors can use in managing a global portfolio, discusses the analytical tools that apply to derivatives, and explains the risk measures used for dynamic hedging. Investors should analyze the costs and benefits of each hedging strategy and focus on how each instrument affects total portfolio risk. Analyzing risk from the perspective of the total portfolio, by using value-at-risk analysis, allows one to understand the links between the returns and risk exposures of individual securities or currencies, portfolios, an institution's total assets and liabilities, and specific derivatives.

Swaps and Their Applications

Various instruments are available to investors who want to manage exposure in global fixed-income and equity securities. Forward contracts, options, and futures have standardized features, such as contract size, maturity, and settlement, that offer investors a convenient way to hedge broad-based or generic currency exposures. Structured notes, swaps, and swap-

tions not only help investors control interest rate and currency risk but also provide customized structures and terms to create or manage unique exposures for specific portfolios. These instruments—especially swaps—allow investors to alter existing cash flows into a desired structure, decrease effective borrowing costs, enhance returns, speculate on interest rate and currency movements, and synthetically access otherwise unavailable or not easily accessible markets.

Cross-Currency Swaps. Most generic swaps are cross-currency swaps. Unlike plain-vanilla interest rate swaps, a currency swap involves two different currencies; therefore, an actual exchange of cash flows based on current spot rates takes place on the origination date and termination date of the currency swap. For example, **Figure 1** shows Counterparty A receiving US$10 million and paying Counterparty B ¥1 billion on the origination date. (For simplicity, this example assumes the yen/dollar exchange rate to be 100.) The termination date may range from three months to 10 years. Because two currencies are involved, the relevant interest rates can be expressed as either fixed or floating and based in either or both currencies. In this example, the swap tenor is two years and Counterparty A pays the U.S. dollar fixed-rate coupon and receives the yen fixed-rate coupon. Because the rates are fixed, a swap of two fixed payments occurs at the end of the term. Thus, in addition to the final interest payment, Counterparty A will pay US$10 million and receive ¥1 billion from Counterparty B on the termination date.

Although this example uses a fixed rate for conceptual reasons, the interest rate on one leg of the

Figure 1. Generic Cross-Currency Swap

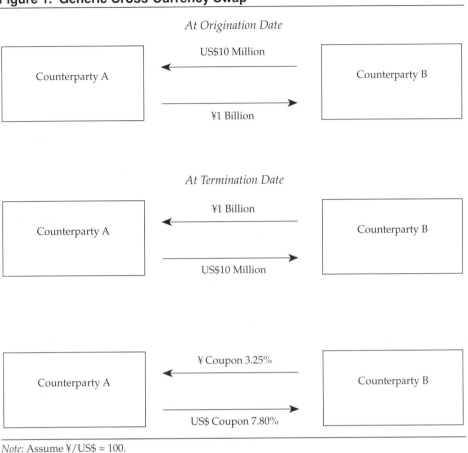

At Origination Date

Counterparty A ← US$10 Million — Counterparty B
Counterparty A → ¥1 Billion → Counterparty B

At Termination Date

Counterparty A ← ¥1 Billion — Counterparty B
Counterparty A → US$10 Million → Counterparty B

Counterparty A ← ¥ Coupon 3.25% — Counterparty B
Counterparty A → US$ Coupon 7.80% → Counterparty B

Note: Assume ¥/US$ = 100.

swap can float, and once the rate floats, the swap becomes cash adjusting. The underlying term structure for pay fixed/receive floating swaps is the LIBOR curve, so a currency swap with a floating-rate leg calls for the exchange of a fixed rate in a foreign currency for U.S. dollar LIBOR. Thus, in another example, Counterparty C might pay U.S. dollar LIBOR and Counterparty D might pay the yen fixed-coupon rate.

Often, such a currency swap becomes a kind of hedging instrument. If investors or corporate finance managers already have yen and know that they will need yen in the future to meet a yen-based obligation, they may enter into a currency swap, similar to a forward agreement, and have the swap termination date coincide with the date on which the yen-based obligation is due.

The key is to think of swaps in a total-return context and in terms of the risk–return trade-off. This approach begins to approximate the value-at-risk approach and forces the investor to look at total portfolio risk. So, instead of thinking of this swap as hedging, the better approach is to think of it as simply part of managing total return.

Once the swap agreement has been executed, one should think in terms of expected return and risk. That is, after the initial exchange is executed, the best approach is to analyze the future payments. This cross-currency swap is basically exposure to two zero-coupon bonds—a short position in a U.S. zero-coupon bond and a long position in a yen zero-coupon bond. In effect, Counterparty A has sold a zero-coupon U.S. dollar bond and bought a zero-coupon yen bond; that is, two years from now, Counterparty A will receive a principal and interest payment in yen. To put this example in terms of a risk–return trade-off, suppose that you are long a yen bond. If the yen interest rate decreases, the value of the yen bond increases; if the yen interest rate increases, the value of the yen bond decreases. The reverse is true if you are short a U.S. dollar bond: When the U.S. interest rate goes up, you benefit; when the rate falls, you suffer.

Thus, counterparties in this example of a currency swap face three sources of risk: yen interest rate risk, U.S. dollar interest rate risk, and currency risk. **Figure 2** illustrates the price surface for a cross-currency swap and depicts the marked-to-market

Figure 2. Price Surface for a Cross-Currency Swap

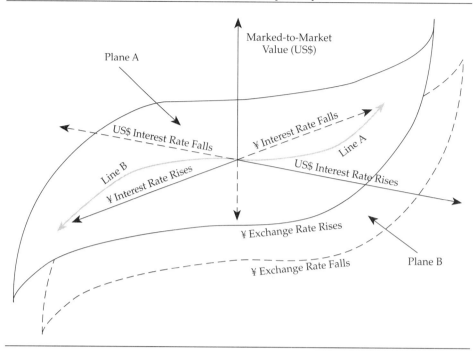

value of the swap (in U.S. dollars) as a function of the U.S. dollar interest rate level, the yen interest rate level, and the exchange rate level. From the perspective of Counterparty A, the value of the swap rises when the U.S. dollar interest rate goes up (the short position) and the value falls when the yen interest rate goes up (the long position). So, when the yen interest rate falls (Line A), Counterparty A makes money and the value of the swap moves upward along Plane A in the direction of Line A. Then, when the yen rates goes up, Counterparty A loses money, and the value of the swap moves downward on Plane A in the direction of Line B. When the dollar interest rate goes up, Counterparty A benefits. When the dollar rate comes down, Counterparty B benefits. When the yen exchange rate falls, then the swap decreases in value, as represented by Plane B.

How an investor thinks in terms of the currency risk now depends on how the investor looks at this swap. If you do the swap and keep the cash (remember, the swap was initially in cash), you will be indifferent to the exchange rate movements, because the yen cash you hold will offset the future yen obligation. So, if you simply opt to keep the yen cash position, you will have no currency exposures.

You could manage your cash position differently, however, and unwind all those positions. In this example, you initially received US$10 million, but if you used the US$10 million, you can forget that ¥1 billion exposure because you have already hedged it away. You are now exposed to the exchange rate

risk. So, because you are holding a zero-coupon yen bond in this trade, you benefit when the yen rate rises. The value is higher when the yen rate rises and lower when the yen rate falls because you have the yen exposure.

Cancel Swaptions. A cancel swaption gives the buyer of the swaption the right to terminate an underlying currency swap that exchanges either a fixed or floating rate in different currencies. If the investor ignores the initial exchange of cash and marks the swap to market, the investor's swap book is long yen bonds and short the U.S. dollar. If the investor sells the swaption, the investor offers the counterparty the right to cancel the underlying swap at any time. What does that offer mean? The counterparty will cancel the swap when the seller makes too much money. When the swap is marked to market, if the value of the swap goes sufficiently high, the counterparty will cancel the swap and cut out the seller's upside return.

The way a cancel swaption works is straightforward. The diagram is shown in **Figure 3.** For example, Counterparty B has the right to cancel the swap. At the strike price, Counterparty B can eliminate the upside returns of Counterparty A when the yen interest rate falls or the U.S. dollar interest rate rises. As with the cross-currency swap, when the yen exchange rate falls, the swaption declines in value, as represented by Plane B. The price surface depicts the value of the swap as a function of the yen interest rate level and the U.S. dollar interest rate level. The

Figure 3. Price Surface for a Cross-Currency Swaption

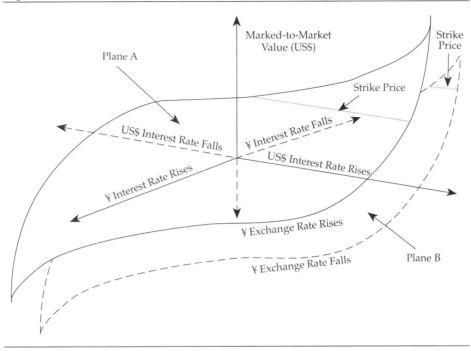

positive (negative) value of the swap means that the swap has positive (negative) marked-to-market value for the holder of the swap position.

This representation assumes no volatility or intrinsic value. With volatility, all the sharp corners will become a smooth surface. Of course, when the counterparty has the option to cancel the swap, you charge a higher interest rate to pay for the option to cancel the swap. The higher interest charged on the yen rate allows the price surface to shift up a bit, although part of the curve is chopped off. A good approach is to intuitively think through how each swap moves up or down with the change in interest rates. Of course, the premium of the option depends on the life of the option and the underlying bond or swap. The longer the maturity of the bond or the swap, the higher the option value.

Rainbow Swaps. The most general rainbow swap is a rainbow swap with *n* colors. This swap can come in a variety of colors, ranging from a swap that delivers the best or worst of *n* assets or currencies to a swap that delivers either the call or put on the maximum or minimum of *n* risky assets or currencies. In a typical rainbow swap, the fixed-rate receiver or payer has the right at each payment date to receive interest payments based in different currencies—the U.S. dollar, German mark, or Japanese yen. Because of the embedded option(s) in this swap, there is a premium paid at origination or the pay-fixed rate is adjusted for the value of the embedded option. The other leg of the swap simply floats off LIBOR, which

is almost like borrowing cash. The focus should be on the leg of the swap that gives the counterparty the right to pay interest or receive interest on the notional amount in one of three or four currencies—that is, the rainbow.

People enter into a rainbow swap to speculate on the relative outperformance of various currencies and/or interest rates. For example, Thai baht interest rates in November 1997 were very high. So, a fixed-rate receiver on a rainbow swap that included the Thai baht enjoyed high income at then-current exchange rates because the interest rate in nominal terms, isolated from the exchange rate movement, looked high. But because the Thai baht was a weak currency, the counterparty did not want to lock into a swap receiving Thai baht interest for the next five years in case the Thai baht exchange rate were to deteriorate further. If things go bad, the fixed-rate receiver can switch to a stronger currency or at least a standard currency, such as the yen, which has a more liquid market than the baht.

This option to select another currency on which interest payments are based is the attractiveness of the rainbow swap. Counterparties agree on several currencies, and every time the interest payment date comes along, the fixed-rate receiver chooses in which currency to receive the current payment.

In terms of the basic building blocks of swaps, the rainbow swap is no different from, for example, being short the U.S. dollar and long the yen. Although long in yen, the investor has a delivery option of switching to other currencies as interest payments come due. Changing the exchange rate, or interest rate in another currency, effectively represents a delivery option built on top of the currency swap.

In addition to the delivery option, an investor could also add a cancellation option, because at some point the investor might want to cancel it. This cancellation option would increase in value as the volatility of various currencies increased.

Basket Swaptions. Many international portfolio managers want to buy baskets of currencies to diversify among various currencies. Basket swaptions accomplish this objective. For example, the buyer of a basket swaption has the option to enter into a swap in which the buyer receives fixed-rate interest payments based on a basket of currencies and pays LIBOR. This arrangement is similar to buying an international portfolio index. Suppose you presently have a U.S. dollar-based bond portfolio and you want to create an international portfolio. Instead of buying all the stocks and bonds, a basket swaption allows you to buy a ratio of various currencies and receive the return on those currencies. In addition, an embedded cancel swaption within the swap allows the fixed-rate receiver to cancel the swap at any time.

Differential Swaps. The differential swap is a hybrid instrument designed to enable counterparties to speculate on interest rate differentials among currencies without directly holding foreign securities and incurring any foreign currency exposure. A counterparty may receive or pay the difference or spread between a long rate and a short rate or the spread between short rates in two countries.

The differential swap is of interest to many international investors because, in many countries, changes in the central bank's monetary policy drive the yield curve. The yield curve in international markets can be somewhat unusual because short-term interest rates can be artificially high or low. For example, in the past, Italy and Germany have had U-shaped yield curves or very steep yield curves for long periods. So, one investment strategy is to focus on how long the investor will remain at a certain point on the yield curve, keeping the maturity of the bond constant over a period of time. The strategy focuses on profiting from the spread between long-term and short-term interest rates or short-term rates in two currencies.

For example, a two-year differential swap in which Counterparty A receives the 10-year constant-maturity Treasury (CMT) rate minus a margin of x basis points (bps) and pays Counterparty B three-month LIBOR is simply the difference between the long-term rate and short-term rates. Counterparty A

enters into this swap because Counterparty A believes the shape of the yield curve will remain unchanged.

This swap can be wrapped in an accrual note. In an accrual note, every quarter, the investor of the note receives a coupon based on the spread. For example, if the spread is more than 1.25 percent, the interest is LIBOR plus 2 percent, but if the spread is less, the interest rate is fixed at a low rate. It is only 1 percent each day for a spread lower than 1.25 percent. If the betting range is only 1.20 percent, Counterparty A gets more money—LIBOR plus 2 percent. If it is less than 1.20 percent, Counterparty A will receive less money. On a price surface for this swap, as shown in **Figure 4**, one source of risk will be the 10-year CMT and the other dimension is the LIBOR rate. As the spread widens—that is, when LIBOR falls and the 10-year CMT rate increases—the value of the swap dramatically increases.

Thus, investors can look at each country's yield curve, estimate whether interest rates are artificially high or low in relation to one another, estimate whether the current shape of the yield curve (steep or inverted) will persist, and then design a differential swap to capture the particular rate view.

Quanto Structured Notes. A quanto structured note allows the participant to benefit from anticipated movements in a price index of some financial asset and insulates the participant from any adverse currency moves related to the index itself. The floating index is based on a separate currency from which the cash flow comes. Typically, the note includes a guaranteed minimum redemption.

For example, if the German mark yield curve were unusually U-shaped, to make money on this unusual market condition, an investor would want to buy the long-term mark bond, short the middle-term bond, and buy the short-term bond to capture the shape and arbitrage against the shape of the curve. If an investor bought mark bonds to capture this trade, however, the investor would automatically face currency risk. In that case, the investor would have to unwind or hedge the currency risk.

The quanto allows this investor to execute the trade synthetically while avoiding or totally ignoring currency risk. In this example, the investor would be paid German mark interest rates in U.S. dollars. Even though the yield curve is based on the mark, the German rate is a U.S. dollar rate. It is an index, and the investor bets this index and gets paid everything in U.S. dollars.

The quanto applies not only to interest rates. Similar to an equity warrant, which is a long-term option written by an institution with a payoff tied to the performance of a stock index, a quanto can provide exposure to a stock index but not the currency. For example, the chosen index might be the

Figure 4. Structure of a Differential Swap

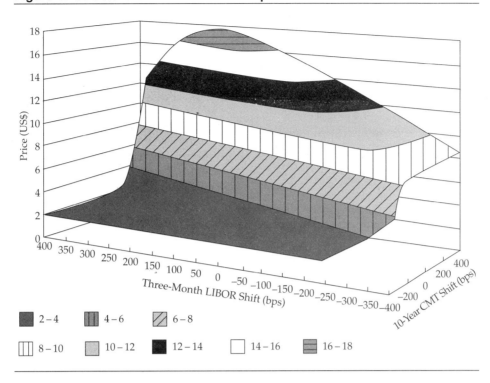

Legend:
- 2–4
- 4–6
- 6–8
- 8–10
- 10–12
- 12–14
- 14–16
- 16–18

(Axes: Price (US$); Three-Month LIBOR Shift (bps); 10-Year CMT Shift (bps))

Nikkei. In this case, if the Nikkei goes up, the quanto investor gets the percentage change of the Nikkei index in U.S. dollars. The quanto has nothing to do with the yen.

As a product, quanto structured notes are easy to understand, but the valuation is not so obvious. Although firms build models for interest rate and currency pricing, for the quanto, the index value has nothing to do with the domestic currency. In terms of valuation, the investor is betting on some index number, which is a different risk source. So, the firms selling quantos have to make use of currency to hedge the exposure. The firms cannot simply use the Black–Scholes option-pricing model applied to an index; they must adjust for the risk premium involved because the quanto is really about making bets on an index number or value. The problem is how to make that transition. If an investor bets on yen bond interest rates and actually pays yen, the investor can go to the yen market and buy that yen bond. The solution is not so obvious for betting on yen interest rates and paying U.S. dollars, because now the investor has to unwind the exchange rate.

Power Note. Power notes are structured notes that pay a coupon linked to a power or multiple of an underlying index rate. An investor in a power note wants to obtain extremely high returns from small changes in the reference rate or index rate over short periods of time. Rather than have a huge principal

amount, the power note effectively increases the interest rate bet by multiplying or compounding the floating-rate index. Thus, a small change in LIBOR produces a large change in the coupon, which increases the interest rate bet. Investors can actually create a mathematical formula for the index on which they want to trade. If an investor multiplies the index by two or three times, the investor creates more convexity to pick up a much higher return. The downside risk of the power note structure is that when the index rate rises, the formula causes the coupon or payoff to exhibit negative convexity and decrease rapidly toward zero. The notional amount of a power swap or the principal amount of a power note has less and less meaning because the investor may be betting three or four times more than the given notional or principal amount. To tie up or forgo other trades or risk exposure as measured by the notional amount is less meaningful when power notes are used to multiply and increase leverage.

Risk Measures for Dynamic Hedging

As more and more derivative instruments make their way into a portfolio, the risk of the total portfolio changes. All of these derivative applications represent long and short positions in various bonds, interest rates, currencies, indexes, and options, which makes the portfolio risk difficult to understand.

Figuring out how to compare these instruments or how to assemble them into a portfolio is complicated, but several analytical tools—including key-rate duration and key-rate convexity—can help decompose each instrument's risk sources. These measures will become the basic building blocks to risk management at the total portfolio level.

◉ Key-Rate Duration. The first consideration is key-rate duration, which measures the price sensitivity of the instrument to key rates. For example, for a cross-currency swap that essentially represents a long position in a yen bond and a short position in a U.S. dollar bond, the risk exposure is sensitivity along the yen curve and sensitivity along the U.S. dollar curve. Key-rate duration is an extension of the single-factor duration and represents the price sensitivity of a bond or swap to changes in key rates.[1] The formula is

$$D_i = \frac{P - P^*}{P \Delta r_i},$$

where

D_i = the key-rate duration for the ith rate
P = price of the instrument
P^* = price of the instrument with a small shift of the interest rate
Δr_i = the basis point change in the specified key rate

Instead of thinking in terms of how a bond value changes by a parallel shift up or down the whole yield curve, investors should think about the sensitivity of the derivative security to different points along the yield curve. All the key rates—three month, one year, two year, three year—can be defined along the relevant yield curve. For a one-year yen–dollar cross-currency swap, the investor would analyze the sensitivity of the swap to the yen yield curve and U.S. dollar yield curve. To calculate the risks along each yield curve, the investor would shock the yen one-year swap rate and the U.S. dollar one-year swap rate by 100 bps up and down and notice how much the swap value changed.

After each key-rate duration for a multiyear swap or bond has been calculated, the investor can find the effective duration of the swap or bond, which is simply the sum of all the key-rate durations:

$$\frac{\Delta P}{P} = -D_1 \Delta r_1 - D_2 \Delta r_2 - \ldots - D_n \Delta r_n,$$

in which each $D_n \Delta r_n$ represents a source of risk along the relevant yield curve. So, a 10-year swap has 10 key rates or 10 risk sources along the yield curve. One can think of Δr_1 as a shift in the 1-year rate, Δr_2 as a shift in the 2-year rate, and so on up to Δr_{10}, the shift in the 10-year rate.

[1] For detailed discussion of key-rate duration, see Thomas S.Y. Ho, "Key Rate Durations: Measures of Interest Rate Risks," *Journal of Fixed Income* (September 1992):29–44.

Given any bond, currency swap, or swaption, an investor can calculate the key-rate durations, add them all up, and determine the effective duration of that instrument. So, key-rate duration is a very useful concept that basically decomposes the effective duration of the swap or bond into its sensitive components.

Next, the investor measures price sensitivity along each yield curve. Key-rate duration allows the portfolio manager to analyze sensitivity to interest rate changes along the yield curve. For the two-year cross-currency swap, a computer model can easily determine the key-rate durations along the yen and the U.S. dollar yield curves. This swap really represents a long position in a two-year yen bond and a short position in a two-year U.S. dollar bond. For example, if the one-year rate of the yen curve shifts up, the value of the swap for the counterparty receiving ¥1 billion on the termination date will fall. If the one-year rate on the U.S. curve moves up and the two-year yen curve rate remains unchanged, the swap value rises. From this perspective, this swap will have two sets of key-rate durations, two key rates for the yen bond (the long position) and then two key rates for the U.S. dollar bond (the short position). Remember that the swap value depends on the positions held. The value to Counterparty A is the negative value to Counterparty B.

The investor can use dynamic hedging to manage the exposure to each key rate. This procedure—whether for a differential swap or a power note—shocks the curve and calculates the sensitivity along the yen curve and the U.S. dollar curve. It provides the portfolio manager with the estimated exposure for each derivative. If the sensitivity to yen and U.S. dollar curves is known, the investor can buy or sell yen bonds or U.S. bonds to hedge each key rate. A portfolio manager can also create a total portfolio with zero sensitivities along all the curves hedged.

Portfolio managers can derive a key-rate duration profile along all the yield curves and determine their exposure to all currencies, which represents the exposure to the entire portfolio. Then, if they want to put a hedge on, they know exactly the positions needed to hedge the exposure of each position. In fact, the trading desk usually takes this disciplined approach to the entire book of business, which requires systematically looking at the total exposure to each yield curve and to each currency.

Delta-Normal Method. The beauty of calculating the key-rate-duration sensitivity is that after it is calculated, only one step remains before one can calculate the value at risk (VAR). This step involves pulling all the risk sources together in the following equation:

$$\Delta P = -\sum_i P D_i \Delta r_i.$$

This equation represents the dollar duration or the dollar level of exposure for a given interest rate change. Thus, the total exposure is the dollar exposure sensitivity to each risk source. If the exposure sensitivity follows a normal distribution and has a known correlation, only simple statistics are needed to estimate the 1 percent alpha, or the 99 percent confidence interval.

The volatility of a portfolio's dollar exposure, or VAR, is calculated by using

$$VAR = \alpha\sigma(\Delta P)\sqrt{\Delta t}.$$

To calculate the standard deviation of the entire portfolio is no more than calculating the standard deviation of each component of the portfolio.

In dynamic hedging, if the sensitivities are calculated to get the correlation of all the risk sources, the result is the VAR calculation. This methodology is called the delta-normal approach, and it has this transparent property that allows a portfolio manager to see the risk exposures, or risk pockets. A risk manager takes the individual risk exposures and builds them into the correlation matrix to get a VAR number for the portfolio.

One concern people have with the delta-normal approach is that the risk is nonlinear. Thus, the VAR is directly proportional to the standard deviation of the risk driver. VAR analysis using Monte Carlo simulation deals with the nonlinear risk of stock options and interest rate options. It can even be extended to capture convexity or the second order effect of interest rate changes, which creates delta and gamma. Therefore, an analyst not only can measure the VAR directly proportional to the volatility but can also capture how VAR would change in a nonlinear relationship to the volatility.

Key-Rate Convexity. After measuring the price sensitivity of the security to key rates, the investor can measure key-rate convexity. Measuring convexity means determining the curvature of the risks. Key-rate convexity is a way of taking the nonlinear relationships of all the key rates and bringing them together in one consistent way in the form of a matrix. The yield curve has different risk sources—one-year rate, two-year rate, three-year rate, four-year rate—and the combination of changes in these risks creates the gamma, or the convexity.

For calculating international risk sources, in which exchange rates and different yield curves must be faced, analysts have the following equation:

$$\frac{\Delta P}{P} = -\text{Duration } \Delta r + \frac{1}{2}\text{Convexity } (\Delta r)^2.$$

The calculation for the portfolio becomes a matrix equation instead of a simple equation, but the idea is the same. The point is that this methodology can be extended to deal with the nonlinearity of derivatives to calculate the whole curvature of the surface, and the VAR analysis can be calculated from the curvature.

One concern people have with dynamic hedging is that focusing on the delta alone requires investors to constantly revise their positions. In dynamic hedging, the more frequently the estimate of sensitivity is made—daily, weekly, or monthly—the more frequently the investor must revise the hedge dynamically by identifying the underlying embedded options and then buying them. Stabilizing the hedge would be nice. The challenge is to find hedges, using swaps or options, that somewhat stabilize portfolio movement and the value of which will not be greatly affected by market movements. This approach is called static hedging. Static hedging does not require as many customized derivatives as dynamic hedging. The investor can package the basic ones to provide roughly what is needed for the hedging or to replicate the underlying portfolio.

Portfolio Risk Analysis

In assuring that the risks of the various derivative instruments in a portfolio add up to the total risk that the investor intends, the portfolio manager can use a quality assurance methodology. **Table 1** illustrates a tabular format that the manager can fill in and use to compare the various sources of risk—key-rate, basis, prepayment, stock, and credit risk—by instrument. The trick is to break down the currencies in terms of risk type instead of security type. That is, for *x* dollars in U.S. dollar government bonds and corporate bonds, the manager would figure out, by using the sensitivity analysis described earlier, how much risk is interest rate risk, equity market risk, and foreign exchange risk. For example, the manager using Table 1 has two funds, Unit A and Unit B. This table indicates the exposure to all the risk sources and the VAR of each unit. The place to focus on is the VAR of each risk source. The risk contribution becomes the beta of each risk source in relation to the total risk defined as VAR. Breaking down each component of risk provides a VAR contribution estimate for each component; the risks then roll out to the total risk level. Of course, because of the correlations between assets and hedging within the portfolio, the risk exposure of each component does not add up to the total risk. For example, a portfolio may have a US$5 million VAR number, but generally, the sum of the VARs of each risk source will be higher than US$5 million.

Such a table or matrix is helpful because it lays out a clear picture of risk contributions. Whether the instruments are called differential swaps, swaptions, or whatever, does not matter. The quality assurance approach provides the exposure within portfolios and within the whole organization—that is, how the firm's assets and liabilities are organized.

Table 1. Quality Assurance Table

Organization Structure	Key Rate	Basis	Prepayment	Stock	Credit Risk	VAR by Units	Risk Contribution	Diversification Factor	Capital Allocation	Risk-Adjusted Return on Capital
Unit A										
Treasury										
Corporate										
MBS[a]										
Subtotal										
Unit B										
Treasury										
Corporate										
MBS										
Subtotal						Total Risk				
VAR by risk source										
Risk contribution										
Diversification factor										
Return attribution										

aMBS = mortgage-backed securities.

This risk contribution approach is particularly useful for international portfolios because one of the main reasons investors go into international portfolios is diversification. So, if investors put a certain amount of money in yen currency, they want to know what the portfolio's real exposure is. The more currencies investors are exposed to, and the less correlated the currencies are, the smaller the contribution to total risk. In yen, for example, the VAR can be US$10 million but the contribution can be US$1 million because much of that US$10 million is diversified across other currencies. The diversification factor takes into account the correlation between currency risk and yield-curve risk. The VAR calculations also take those risks into account, and the contribution risk thus can be identified.

All this analysis can be used to assemble a comprehensive analysis of a portfolio on a particular date. **Table 2** groups market values and various sources of risk—equity, interest rate, foreign exchange—by currencies for a hypothetical portfolio. In this example, the functional currency is the Swedish krona and the total German mark exposure is a short position of about DM8 billion. Table 2 shows how the values of each instrument roll up to total market value. The market value by currencies is additive, but the VAR calculation is not additive. Everything has to be recalculated. Recalculating the total risk shows how much risk gets diversified or hedged away as the information rolls up. This approach shows how each item adds risk to the portfolio's total risk exposure.

Conclusion

The presentation has now come full circle. It began with discussion of various derivative applications, such as cross-currency swaps and power notes, with a focus on the opportunities to use them and their applications. Putting these instruments in a portfolio requires understanding the risk of each instrument and examining the exposures in terms of their contribution to overall portfolio risk.

Investors need to know the risk contribution from each source because, then, they can decide what derivatives they need to manage overall exposure. Looking at the total portfolio first is the most effective way to analyze risk. If a particular derivative is chosen for the specific impact it is expected to have or to achieve a particular strategy but the manager has not looked first at the big picture, that derivative's effect might be washed out by another product. A narrowly focused derivative can have exactly the impact that is needed. The task is to look at the actual contribution of each source to risk and how each source contributes to return and then to define a swap or other derivative that does the job on that level without overhedging. Many investors overhedge because they look at only one unit. Looking at the whole portfolio protects against overhedging most of the time. Risk starts at the level of each security and rolls up to the whole portfolio. Determining risk at the portfolio level leads to action, which leads back to the security level as the investor decides which derivative can be bought to manage total portfolio risk.

Table 2. Portfolio Evaluation, May 30, 1995

Currency/Source of Risk	Market Value by Assets (Swedish krona)	Market Value by Currencies (Swedish krona)	Total Market Value (Swedish krona)	Delta-Normal VAR (Swedish krona)
German mark		−8,029,512,802.05	−3,771,365,237.04	
Equity	207,413,697.67			13,064,580.25
Interest rate	−8,820,409,119.72			36,982,892.51
Foreign exchange	583,482,620.00			26,240,827.60
French franc		11,874,907,355.40		
Equity	171,906,626.36			14,486,777.48
Interest rate	10,675,260,729.04			37,326,375.08
Foreign exchange	1,027,740,000.00			44,290,663.77
British pound		−4,526,830,517.34		
Equity	197,266,694.30			10,685,110.97
Interest rate	−4,136,817,211.64			31,896,956.22
Foreign exchange	587,280,000.00			23,107,028.34
Japanese yen		12,862,868,409.32		
Equity	143,010,038.87			12,089,772.07
Interest rate	11,838,938,370.45			14,800,453.31
Foreign exchange	880,920,000.00			52,651,722.16
U.S. dollar		−15,952,797,682.36		
Equity	165,273,815.63			6,870,169.86
Interest rate	−14,212,698,157.99			23,458,545.87
Foreign exchange	−1,905,373,340.00			0.00

Question and Answer Session

Thomas S.Y. Ho

Question: On an empirical basis, which risk source tends to be the most important, or does importance depend on the nature of the portfolio?

Ho: The importance of a risk source very much depends on the nature of the portfolio. It also depends on the philosophy of the portfolio. For example, if you want to be diversified internationally, you face currency risk. If your investment strategy is based purely on interest rates, you will hedge all the currency risk. Other strategies have a lot of interest rate risk because portfolios can be leveraged. People borrow a lot of money and buy securities, so even though interest rates do not move much, exposure can be high.

Question: Do you believe VAR measures risk accurately, or is something else coming on the scene that might supersede VAR?

Ho: VAR is a useful tool, and it is a great contribution to our industry because it provides a standardized way of making comparisons. Using VAR as the measure, people can compare the relative risks of different portfolios. Too much emphasis has been placed on what VAR cannot do and not enough on the applications of VAR. It *can* do a lot. I try to demonstrate that VAR offers a straightforward way of showing all the risk exposures in a whole enterprise or portfolio, a feature that has useful implications. The only drawback is that if the numbers are badly calculated and if the instruments are unstable, VAR can give a false sense of security. If the information is accurate, VAR is useful.

Picturing Volatility and Correlation

John Zerolis
Director, Risk Control
Swiss Bank Corporation

The relationship between volatility and correlation can be expressed as a triangle or a tetrahedron—with volatility as a distance and correlation as an angle. Visualizing these shapes clarifies the least understood variable in option-pricing models: volatility. Adding currencies to these triangles or tetrahedrons illustrates how the investor's base currency affects the correlations of returns. The outcome can be creation of a truly optimal portfolio.

In the game of baseball, it is not so much how strong a baseball batter is but how quickly the batter can process visual images; the batter has about one-seventh of a second to determine when and where the ball will arrive. People develop the innate ability to process pictures quickly at an early age and can use it to understand complex mathematics.

Analysts can gain understanding of the possible (and best) uses of derivatives by turning the mathematics into pictures. In this presentation, I will discuss mathematical and quantitative topics in a nonmathematical and nonquantitative way. The presentation first addresses how to decide what to use as volatility in option-pricing models. The presentation then turns to the mathematics of volatility and correlation (particularly when several currencies are involved). After discussing the mathematics, the presentation provides applications of volatility-and-correlation geometry to portfolios and derivatives for portfolios. Because a picture is worth a thousand words, the presentation of material is carried out primarily with diagrams and figures.

Pricing Models

One aspect an analyst needs to consider when deciding on a model for pricing derivatives is how much of a model is really needed. Analysts may choose models with all kinds of bells and whistles but then find they do not have the data to plug in for those parameters or find that the model is simply too complicated for their purposes.

Knowing the assumptions of the model is important to understanding the model's limitations. The adage for computer use also applies to option-pricing models: Garbage in, garbage out. So, analysts need to be very careful about what data they feed into a model.

In terms of quantitative modeling for options and other derivatives, the premier model—a Nobel Prize-winning model—is the Black–Scholes option-pricing model. Most practitioners have some familiarity with the model, either from using it or studying it. The Black–Scholes model is quite interesting because it is more robust than some critics think. In practice, the model and its variations work well (which cannot be said about many models) even in situations where it might be expected not to work. Of course, the model is not perfect.

Inputs to a Black–Scholes option-pricing model include the strike price of the option, the spot price of the underlying security, time to expiration, various interest rate and dividend assumptions, and of course, volatility. In the Black–Scholes model, the theoretical value of the option is, assuming stock prices follow a lognormal distribution, the discounted expected value of the option payout at expiration. **Figure 1** provides the distribution of prices for a stock with an initial price of 100, volatility of 30 percent, and an interest rate, r, of zero. Given the data, one can estimate the probability that the stock price will end up at certain prices after a year. The value of the option—a European call or put option (an option that can be exercised only at the expiration date), for example—is the expected value given that distribution.

Over short periods of time (for example, one month), a lognormal distribution is nearly the same as a normal or Gaussian distribution, as shown in the

Figure 1. Black–Scholes Model

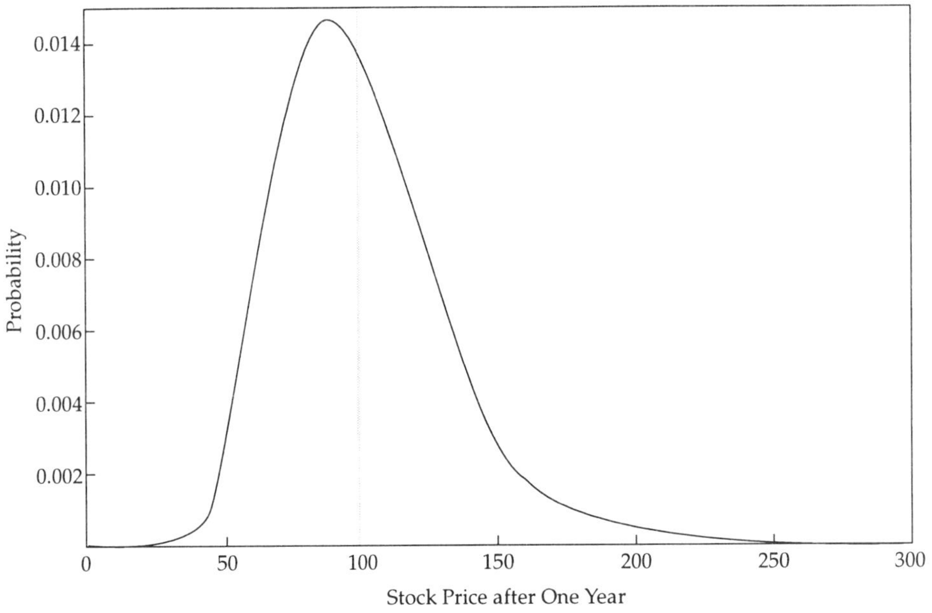

Note: Volatility = 30 percent, initial price = 100, and $r = 0$.

short-term panel of **Figure 2**, but over a longer period, the lognormal distribution takes a different shape, as shown in the long-term panel of Figure 2. A lognormal distribution is the appropriate measure for something that follows a percentage-type process—that is, something that moves in such a way that if one invests twice the amount, one should get twice the return. Given this type of distribution, the instrument is more likely to decrease than to increase in price over a long period of time, but because the distribution is bounded by zero below and is not bounded above, the average will still be 100. Analysts should keep in mind that the lognormal distribution behaves differently from the normal distribution. If analysts assume the distribution for a derivative price is normal, they may wonder why certain things happen to the price of long-dated options.

Volatility. Volatility has a huge impact on the risk and value of a derivative, but volatility is, in a sense, the least understood variable, the one about which analysts have the least certainty, and the least certain of the inputs to option-pricing models. Many opinions exist about how to calculate volatility, but the definition is simple: Volatility is the annualized standard deviation of the natural log of stock returns (σ). When quoted as an annual percentage, volatility is how much one expects the price of the underlying security to increase or decrease (±1 standard deviation for a normal distribution) two-thirds of the time in one year.

Volatility does have a unit: 1 over the square root

of time, $1/\sqrt{\text{Time}}$. So, if the period is two years, the riskiness is not necessarily doubled; the appropriate factor is the square root of 2.

From where does the volatility forecast for a model like the Black–Scholes come? If you take a historical perspective, you use past prices to measure volatility. If you take an event-driven outlook, you predict that something will happen at a specific time to move the price, and therefore, you expect a particular volatility. If you take an implied "efficient market" view, you find out what other analysts with options think volatility will be and use that number. These approaches do not necessarily yield the same number.

The value of a call option is related to both the underlying security price and the volatility. **Figure 3** shows the theoretical value of a European call option (on the y-axis) for three levels of volatility—low (zero or parity), slightly higher (5 percent), and high (15 percent). The underlying price is given on the x-axis. The strike price is 100, and the time to expiration is one year. As the call moves out of the money, the volatility increases, and the price of the call increases. Of course, if the volatility is zero and the call is out of the money, the call is worthless. If the call is in the money, it is worth the difference between the underlying price and the strike price.

Another way of looking at how the value is related to volatility is to consider how the price of the call varies depending on whether the strike is in the money, out of the money, or at the money. **Figure 4**

Figure 2. Lognormal Distribution

Short Term

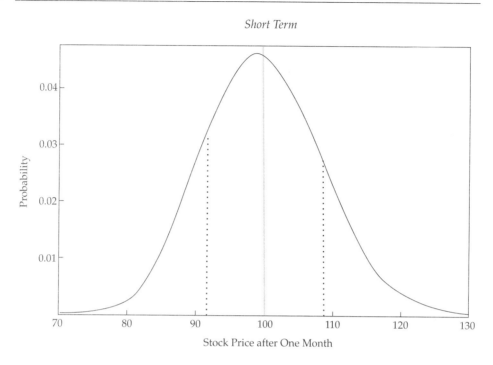

Long Term

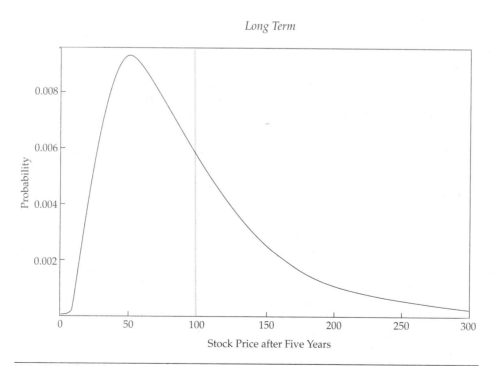

Notes: Volatility = 30 percent, initial price = 100, and r = 0. In the top figure, 109 = the 100 mean + 1 standard deviation. Plus 1 standard deviation equals 9 percent or 30 percent/$\sqrt{12}$.

Figure 3. European Call Option's Theoretical Value for Three Volatilities

Note: Strike = 100; time = one year.

Figure 4. European Call Option's Theoretical Value for Three Strike Prices

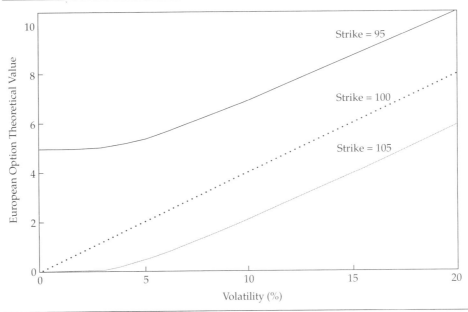

Note: Price = 100; time = one year.

demonstrates the relationship of volatility to value for these three scenarios. If the call is in the money, it has value at zero volatility. If the call is out of the money and has zero volatility, it has zero value. If the call (or put) is at the money, the value of the call is proportional to the volatility. The buyer of an at-the-money call is buying volatility because, as volatility goes up, the price of the at-the-money call goes up.

    ■ *Delta.* The delta (Δ) of an option is the option value's sensitivity to changes in the underlying security price. It can be thought of as how much one would need to hedge in order to hedge the option. **Figure 5** illustrates the concept with a strike price of 100 and standard deviation of 15 percent. When the put is deep in the money, delta is 100 percent. If the put is way out of the money, delta is zero. In between, the delta's behavior depends on the time to expiration. As the time to expiration increases, the curve

Figure 5. Option Value Sensitivity to Price: Delta

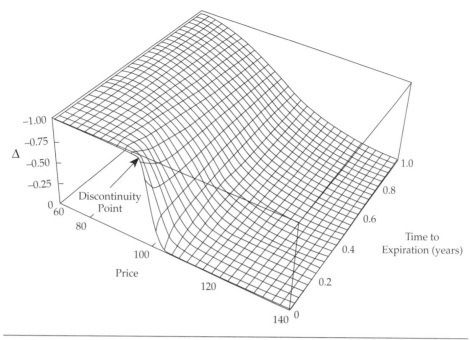

Note: Strike = 100; σ = 15 percent.

becomes smoother. For short-dated options or as the expiration date approaches, the curve is steeper, which reveals a point of discontinuity. At this point, whether the put will move in the money or out of the money is basically a coin toss.

■ *Vega*. The option value's sensitivity to changes in volatility, vega (∂), is another good measure. As illustrated by **Figure 6**, as the time to expiration for an option increases, the value of volatility increases because more time exists for the underlying security to change price and the option to move in the money. Thus, long-dated options are almost always worth more than short-dated options with the same strike price.

Using Measures in Models. In discussing correlation and volatility, distinguishing between a *measure* and a *model* is important. Knowing the volatility and correlation is not enough to constitute a model. This information alone does not provide the price of an instrument, indicate the level of risk, or explain how to hedge the risk. Volatility and correlation are simply parameters in a model.

One of the first concerns in using a model is whether the parameters are appropriate to, or fit, the model. If parameters are used that were intended for a different model, the fit may not be good.

The parameters, or measures, have different meanings. For example, volatility and correlation may be historical volatility and historical correlation,

or they may be implied volatility and implied correlation. Historical values are based in reality; implied values are perceptions. The distinction is important. In pricing options or trading in options, implied volatility is cause for concern. Every other variable—the strike price and the time to expiration—is known. Volatility is much more ambiguous. Implied volatility is simply the number put into the formula to get the price at which the option currently trades.

If you want to measure perception, then you want to calculate implied volatility and correlation and measure traded option prices. If you want to measure reality, then you want to use historical data for correlation and volatility and use traded prices on the underlying security. If you want to predict perceptions, then you want to forecast implied volatility and correlation and predict future option prices. If you want to predict reality—what will happen to correlations in the next six months or to volatilities in the next year—hedging risk, or delta hedging, becomes important.

Model Limitations. Option-pricing models are useful; they provide insights, and they allow analysts to price, hedge, and so on. But the limitations of the models need to be understood. The fact that computers can do many things with great precision does not eliminate a model's limitations. For example, computers allow the theoretical value and the delta of a European option to be computed to a thousand decimal

Figure 6. Option Value Sensitivity to Volatility: Vega

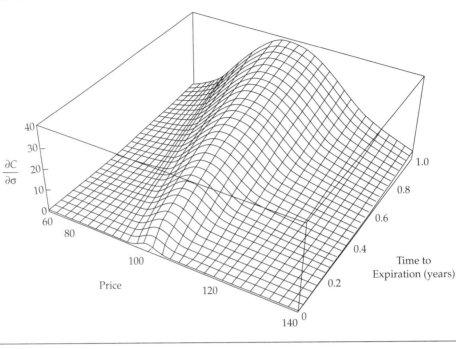

Note: Strike = 100; σ = 15 percent.

places. But simply because a number can be computed with extreme precision does not mean that reality will hold to that digit. The computer does not set limitations; the reality of what is being modeled does.

Similarly, lognormal density functions allow an analyst to compute the likelihood, assuming the market has a certain annual volatility, that the market will move in a certain direction or by a certain percentage in one day. The answer is expressed as the average number of years one would have to wait to see a move of a specific size. For example, with 20 percent volatility, a 1 percent move would likely occur in 0.0185 year—about once a week, which is typical of equity volatility. The U.S. equity market would actually be slightly lower, so for that market, for a 1 percent move, one would expect to wait approximately a week, which is reasonable. The computations if the underlying process is lognormal stay reasonable for small moves, but what happens when the move is –10 percent? The computations say that, if the markets are lognormal, a –10 percent move will occur about once in 122 trillion years. How realistic is that prediction: The universe is thought to be roughly 17 billion years old, but a –10 percent move occurs only every 122 trillion years? Obviously, a –10 percent move has happened. The markets have experienced even a 20 percent move. So, the lognormal distribution calculation may be good enough for small moves, but for the extreme moves, a lognormal distribution is not good

enough. For this reason, any risk or pricing mechanism should include the notion of stress testing.[1]

Currency. The impact of currencies on investments is a key part of measuring volatility and correlation. Much confusion surrounds the issue of currencies, the impact of currencies on investments, and how currency is connected to measuring volatility.

Currency matters because returns matter. The actual returns depend on the currency in which something is priced because returns are percentage changes in prices. To a U.S. investor, a 10 percent U.S. dollar return is not the same as a 10 percent Japanese yen return. Because volatility is the volatility of the security's returns—the amount plus or minus within which you would expect returns to fall two-thirds of the time over the course of one year—the volatility depends on the currency.

Analysts care not only about returns but also about how those returns are correlated, and the correlations between currencies, products, or anything else depend on the currency in which they are measured.

Volatility-and-Correlation Geometry

The close relationship between volatility and correlation can be expressed as a "volatility-and-correlation

[1]See Maarten Nederlof's presentation, pp. 73–81.

triangle." Let σ_{AB} represent the cross-volatility of A and B (the annualized standard deviation of returns of B measured in terms of A) and $_A\rho_{BC}$ represent the correlation between B and C with respect to A; that is, the correlation between the returns of B measured in A and the returns of C measured in A (the subscript to the left of ρ is thus the currency of measurement). **Figure 7** illustrates the volatility and correlation triangle using the U.S. dollar (USD), Japanese yen (JPY), and British pound sterling (GBP).

Volatility, σ, is expressed as a distance, a length, using any unit as long as the same unit is used to measure each volatility. The length of each volatility is used to assemble the triangle.

Then, the correlations are the cosines of each angle. For example, the correlation between the yen and the pound as measured from a U.S. dollar-based perspective ($_{USD}\rho_{GBP,JPY}$) is measured by the cosine of the angle opposite the volatility one is measuring ($\sigma_{GBP,JPY}$).

In other words, the relationships of volatilities and correlations in various currencies can be represented by pictures that are equivalent to exact mathematical equations. Once the triangle is set up, one can determine the correlation and volatility from the perspective of every other currency. The triangle provides a global perspective on correlation and volatility.

To compute the correlations for the triangle, one needs to remember what a cosine is and translate degrees into units of correlation. **Figure 8** provides a "correlation protractor" that converts degrees into correlation coefficients. For example, an angle of 0 degrees translates into a correlation of +1.0, an angle of 90 degrees translates into a correlation of 0.0, and an angle

of 180 degrees translates into a correlation of –1.0. All the possible angles are between 0 and 180, and all the possible correlations are between +1 and –1.

In short, correlation and volatility analysis can be done using nothing but a ruler, the protractor, and a piece of paper. **Figure 9** provides an example in U.S. dollars, German marks (DEM), and the U.S. equity market (proxied by the S&P 500 Index, SPX). Suppose the volatility of the U.S. equity market is 16 percent, the volatility of the German mark is 11 percent from a U.S. dollar point of view, and the cross-volatility of the German mark and the U.S. equity market is 19 percent. This example might apply to an outperformance option, an option on U.S. equity struck in German marks. Given those volatilities, the correlations can be determined by measuring the angles formed by the three lengths (volatilities) and using the correlation protractor to translate the angles into correlation coefficients. As Figure 9 shows, from a U.S. dollar point of view, the German mark's correlation with the U.S. equity market is nearly zero; the angle is close to 90 degrees (that is, the correlation between SPX and DEM valued in USD is cos[87.4°] = 0.045). From a German mark investor's point of view, however, the U.S. dollar and the U.S. equity market are correlated; the angle is about 60 degrees, which is about a 0.54 correlation (that is, the correlation between SPX and USD valued in USD is cos[57.3°] = 0.541). The fact that, from a U.S. dollar point of view, the German mark should not be related to the U.S. equity market but that, from a German mark point of view, the U.S. dollar should be related to the U.S. equity market might be perplexing if viewed simply

Figure 7. Volatility-and-Correlation Triangle

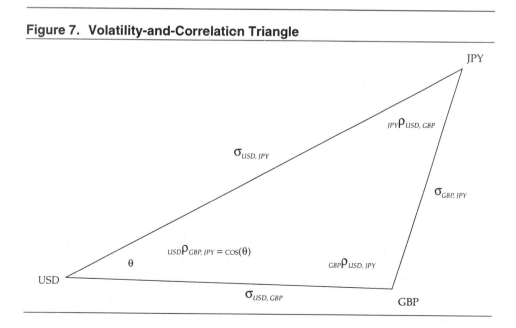

Figure 8. Correlation Protractor

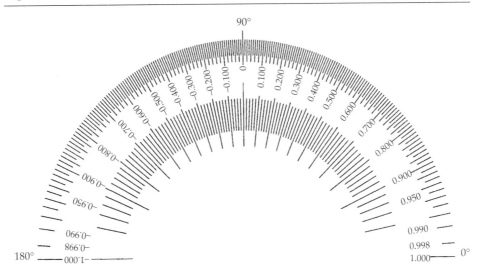

Figure 9. Example Triangle for U.S. Equity Market, U.S. Dollars, and German Marks

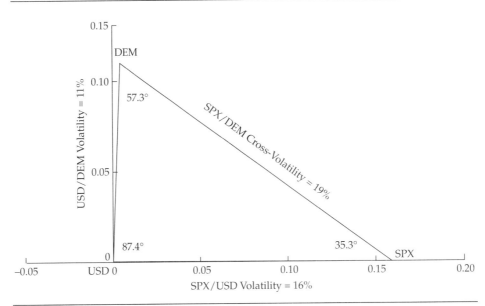

Note: Values provided are for illustration only.

in mathematical terms, but the triangle gives a picture of the same mathematical relationship. Finally, from the U.S. equities market point of view, the German mark and the U.S. dollar are highly correlated (the correlation between DEM and USD valued in SPX is cos[35.3°] = 0.816). Some might question the relevance of knowing what the correlation of marks and dollars is from the U.S. equity market perspective, but if a manager's benchmark is the U.S. equity market, then the U.S. equity market is, in fact, a kind of currency. So, asking how different currencies are correlated relative to this unit of measurement makes

sense for such a manager.

The volatility-and-correlation triangle can also show certain limitations on correlations and volatilities. Certain triangles are simply not possible. For example, volatilities of

$$\left| \sigma_{AC} - \sigma_{BC} \right| \leq \sigma_{AB} \leq \sigma_{AC} + \sigma_{BC}$$

produce the three lengths of volatility on the left of **Figure 10**, which cannot connect to form a triangle. Similarly, a set of correlations cannot produce a triangle with three right angles; such a triangle is an impossibility in Euclidean geometry. Somewhere,

Figure 10. Triangle Impossibilities

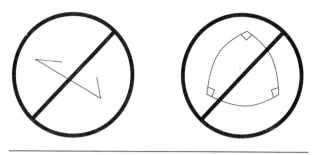

somehow, something has to be correlated, because in financial instruments, absolute zero does not really exist. Together, the correlations must equal

$$\cos^{-1}(_C\rho_{AB}) + \cos^{-1}(_B\rho_{AC}) + \cos^{-1}(_A\rho_{BC})$$
$$= \pi \text{ (i.e., 180 degrees).}$$

So, an analyst may make the assumption that certain correlations are zero, but this assumption cannot be made from the point of view of every currency.

Using the Triangle in Portfolio Management. The triangle can also be used to show how portfolios work. In 1827, August F. Möbius invented *barycentric coordinates*, or coordinates relative to a point. Barycentric coordinates were around for at least 70 years prior to the development of correlation, but they can be used to analyze the correlation and volatility of portfolios. The Möbius system defines locations by weighting points. A new point represents the "center of mass" of weighted points. For example, given

triangle$_{ABC}$, 100 percent A would be a point sitting right at A, 50 percent A and 50 percent B would be a coordinate sitting at the midpoint between A and B, and 75 percent A and 25 percent B would be a point approximately one-fourth the distance from A to B. **Figure 11** illustrates how a new point can be determined by weighting three points. The sum of the weights must equal 1, but the weights do not all have to be positive. For example, point D represents 150 percent in A and –50 percent in B. Point E in the middle of the triangle represents weights of one-third A, one-third B, and one-third C. Every point on the plane can be defined as some weighted combination of the three original points A, B, and C.

The barycentric point can be viewed as a portfolio. For a portfolio, the weights also sum to 1. If currencies and assets are plotted as a triangle, a point somewhere on the same plane represents a portfolio of those assets. The correlations and the volatilities of the portfolio can be read from the angles and distances between points. **Figure 12** shows the portfolio as the point (P) in the middle of the triangle containing a third of each asset (A, B, and C), with the standard deviation, σ_{AP}, shown by the line segment and the correlation, $_A\rho_{PC}$, as the angle.[2]

Once the triangle showing correlations and volatilities has been drawn, an analyst can use the picture to analyze the impact of changes on a particular basket of assets. For example, for the relationships shown in Figure 9, what would the volatility of a

[2]For additional reading on triangulating risk, see John Zerolis, "Triangulating Risk," *Risk* (December 1996).

Figure 11. Barycentric Coordinates

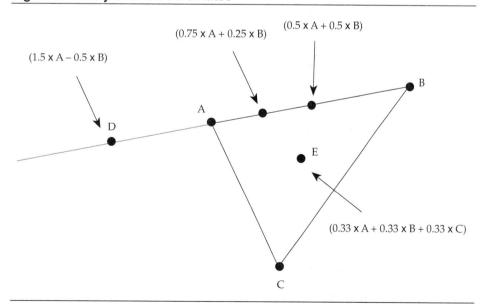

Figure 12. Portfolio Correlations and Volatilities

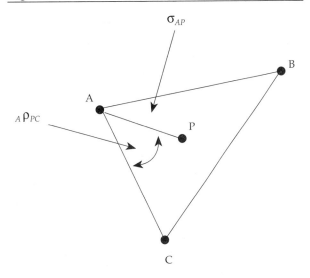

Note: P = 0.33A + 0.33B + 0.33C.

basket with half the investment in German marks and half the investment in U.S. equities be for a U.S. dollar-based investor? If the angles represent the correlations involved, the volatility would be the distance from the USD corner to a midway point on the line opposite that corner basket, the line from SPX to DEM. To find the correlation between that basket and some other asset, one would change the angle and measure the cosine of the new angle.

This concept also applies to measurements made from historical data. For example, an analyst can transpose a scatterplot of U.K. stock returns and the British pound foreign exchange returns, as measured from a U.S. dollar perspective, to a triangle. The U.K. market can be proxied by the Financial Times Stock Exchange (FTSE) Index and the historical returns will be the weekly returns from January 1991 through June 1996. Using only two points and the origin, the analyst can determine the volatilities of the GBP, USD, and FTSE assets and the correlations between those assets, as **Figure 13** shows. The distance from USD to FTSE indicates that the volatility of U.K. stocks is 14.47 percent, the distance from USD to GBP indicates that the volatility of the British pound is about 10.85 percent, and finally, the distance between FTSE and GBP indicates that the volatility of U.K. stocks in terms of British pounds is about 12.67 percent. The correlation between U.K. stock returns and GBP from a USD perspective is the cosine of the USD angle.

An analyst can use the triangle in Figure 13 to decide how to hedge a basket of U.K. equities with British pounds. Trading British pounds for U.S. dollars can be viewed as moving in the direction from GBP to

USD. If the initial portfolio is FTSE, the direction is the same as from FTSE to point A. Therefore, if you want to minimize the "distance" (that is, USD volatility) from U.S. dollars in the portfolio, the figure shows the amount of British pounds you need to trade to barycentrically move the portfolio from FTSE to point A. Thus, hedging a basket of U.K. equities would involve buying dollars with pounds in an amount equal to 71 percent of the value of the FTSE stock position.

Figure 13 also shows that from the point of view of a U.S. dollar-based investor considering FTSE futures trading, the FTSE futures contract and FTSE stock basket are not perfectly correlated. The correlation between them is less than 1 because the futures contract involves a currency, which creates a variation in daily margin, whereas the FTSE index is simply a basket of assets. From a USD perspective, volatility decreases when FTSE futures are used in place of buying the basket of FTSE stocks because of the implicit currency hedge in the futures contract.

From a U.S. dollar view, the stock basket and the British pound each have a certain volatility and there is a certain correlation between them. The FTSE futures contract can be considered to be a combination of these two components, which establishes the particular barycentric point.

The optimal amount needed to minimize the standard deviation of a basket of assets can also be determined from a picture. The histograms in **Figure 14** illustrate that a trade of 71 percent British pounds would minimize the standard deviation of the result-

Figure 13. A Transposed Scatterplot

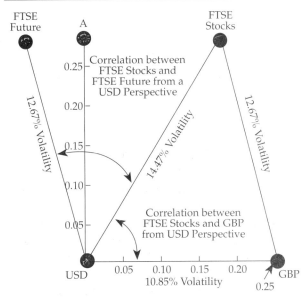

Notes: Triangle from historical data (weekly returns, January 1991 through June 1996); volatilities are annualized. Values provided are for illustration only.

Figure 14. Frequency Histograms: U.K. Equity and British Pound from U.S. Dollar Perspective

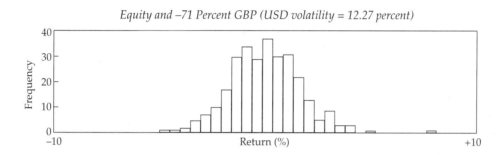

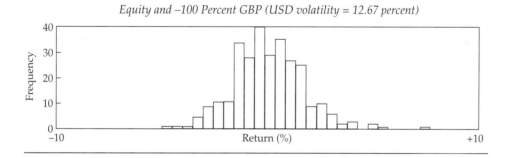

ing returns. The result is based on the data; it does not necessarily depend on being lognormal.

From Triangle to Tetrahedron. When correlations between four sets of returns are involved, a three-dimensional figure is needed. Such a tetrahedron is shown in **Figure 15** for the Swiss franc (CHF), the Japanese yen, the British pound, and the U.S. dollar. The distances still represent the volatilities, and the angles opposite each side represent the correlations between currencies. The most important element is the perspective of the investor. A question about the correlation between the Swiss franc and the British pound must be posed in terms of whether the correlation is viewed from a dollar-based investor's

point of view or from a yen-based investor's point of view. Two angles exist for the correlation between CHF and JPY, and these angles do not have to be equal. Even though the volatility between the Swiss franc and the British pound is the same from any perspective, the correlation depends on the currency perspective from which the correlation is measured.

Table 1 illustrates the importance of the currency perspective. The table contains a correlation matrix calculated from historical data for the U.S. dollar and British pound points of view. The table also shows the pairwise volatility between the two, which reveals the cross-volatilities between those currencies.

The pairwise volatility data can be translated into a tetrahedron by using simple Euclidean geom-

Figure 15. Tetrahedron to Depict Relationships of Four Currencies

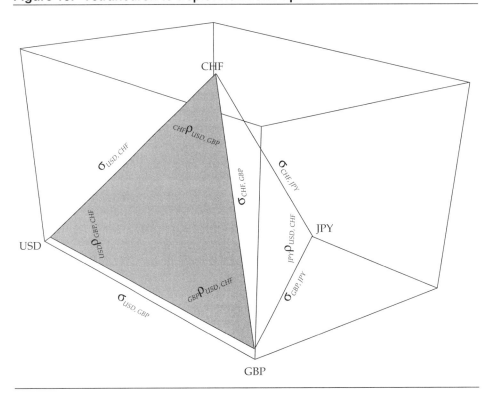

Table 1. Currency Perspective: Correlations and Volatilities

	USD	SPX	FTSE	GBP
Correlation with respect to U.S. dollar				
SPX	—	1.000	0.518	0.073
FTSE	—	0.518	1.000	0.342
GBP	—	0.073	0.342	1.000
Correlation with respect to British pound sterling				
USD	1.000	0.621	0.235	—
SPX	0.621	1.000	0.547	—
FTSE	0.235	0.547	1.000	—
Pairwise volatility				
USD	0	8.94	13.60	7.72
SPX	8.94	0	11.80	11.40
FTSE	13.60	11.80	0	13.10
GBP	7.72	11.40	13.10	0

Note: Values provided are for illustrative purposes only.

etry. The result is the geometric object in **Figure 16**. Four corners exist: a U.S. dollar corner, a U.K. equity market corner, a U.S. equity market corner, and a British pound corner. For a British pound-based investor, three angles exist at the GBP corner. The correlation matrix from a pound investor's point of view is nothing but the cosine of each angle from this corner: To obtain the correlation between the U.S. dollar and the U.S. equity market for a pound-based investor, this investor calculates the cosine of the angle between the GBP and USD corners and the SPX and GBP corners:

$$_{GBP}\rho_{SPX,USD} = \cos\angle_{GBP}$$

The U.S. dollar-based correlation matrix is nothing but the cosine of each angle from the USD corner. To determine the volatilities, the distances are measured. The USD–GBP volatility is the distance between those two corners.

The reason the correlation matrix is different from the perspective of different currencies is clear: because the correlations are determined from the angles of one corner of the geometric object versus the angles from another corner of the same object. Different correlations exist, but they must be consis-

Figure 16. Tetrahedron for Pairwise Volatility

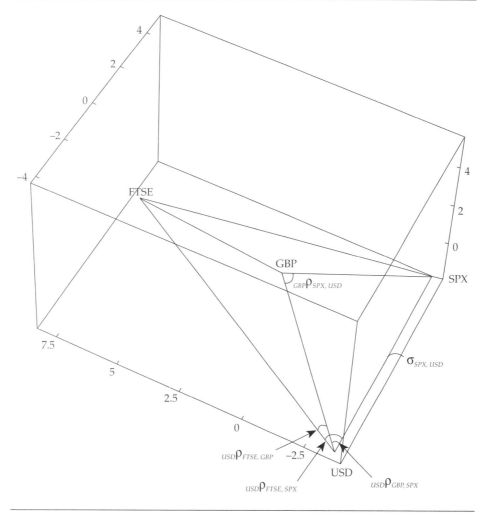

Note: Market returns measured by the Bolsa IPC Index from December 1994 to February 1995.

tent with one another; that is, one angle (correlation) cannot be changed without affecting another angle (correlation). This condition may be tough to understand mathematically, but it is visually intuitive.

Using barycentric coordinates, one can see how the volatility of a basket of assets will depend on the weights of each asset in the portfolio. This relationship between the volatilities of baskets can also be clearly seen in Figure 16. A U.S. dollar-based investor can see that the volatility of a basket of U.S. equities and U.K. equities depends on the weights; the distance (volatility) is measurable and will change if the weights are changed. This approach allows one to take advantage of the correlations between various assets to determine the optimal basket of assets from each currency perspective—that is, the portfolio with the lowest volatility.

Application to Options. Different kinds of op-

tions have different sensitivities to certain parameters. For example, an investor may have a quanto option on a foreign index or an outperformance put or cross-option on a foreign stock index. Although the options may look the same, they behave quite differently. Because a quanto put option hedges an index value, the investor hedges the foreign currency and the foreign equity. The domestic currency has a minor connection to the quanto option, whereas the outperformance put option hedges the U.S. dollar and the foreign equity exposure.

Mexico's devaluation of the peso provides a scenario in which to examine the differences between these options. **Figure 17** shows the relative performance of a quanto put option and an outperformance put option between November 30, 1994, and January 31, 1995. Consider the holder of a quanto put struck at 15 percent below the at-the-money price: In terms of Mexican pesos, this quanto option was only 4

Figure 17. Mexican Equity Returns and Behavior of Two Put Options

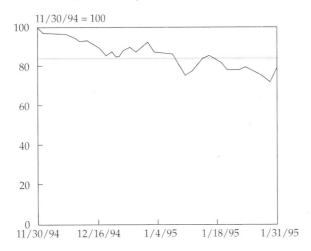

Quanto Put Option in Mexican Pesos

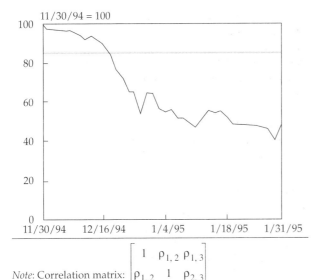

Outperformance Put Option in U.S. Dollars

Note: Correlation matrix: $\begin{bmatrix} 1 & \rho_{1,2} & \rho_{1,3} \\ \rho_{1,2} & 1 & \rho_{2,3} \\ \rho_{1,3} & \rho_{2,3} & 1 \end{bmatrix}$

Source: Based on data from P.J. Rousseeuw, "The Shape of Correlation Matrices," *American Statistician* (August 1994):276–79.

percent in the money. For an outperformance put from a U.S. dollar perspective, however, when the market dropped by 51 percent, the payout would have been 36 percent in U.S. dollar terms. So, analysts need to be aware of the derivative instruments they use to hedge; sometimes, two options that seem similar behave significantly differently.

Validity of the Data. An important issue is

whether the numbers being used in an option-pricing model are valid. For instance, if you have two instruments, you have one correlation that has a valid range between –1 and +1. If you have more than two instruments, you will need a correlation matrix with $[n(n-1)]/2$ correlation coefficients between n assets. So, three correlations require a 3×3 matrix. Consider this exercise: Using a blank piece of paper, draw a dot, and from that dot, draw an arrowhead. Using the same dot, draw another arrow pointing in the opposite direction. Using that same dot, now try to draw a third arrow that is opposite to each of the two you have already drawn. The third arrow does not exist. There is no direction that is mutually opposite to those two you have already drawn.

The two drawn arrows have a correlation of –1. If you could find three arrows that were mutually opposite to each other, the correlation matrix would be –1, –1, –1, and so forth. But because these mutually opposite arrows do not exist, –1, –1, –1, and so forth cannot be a valid correlation matrix. Mathematically, the condition for having a valid matrix is known as *positive semidefinite* (PSD). Eigenvalues can be used to test this condition. If any Eigenvalues are negative, the matrix is not valid. For a 3×3 matrix, three separate correlations are present. Consider an x, y, z cube in which each correlation is an angle. **Figure 18** shows that a cube would exist if every correlation coefficient in a 3×3 correlation matrix could range between –1 and +1; in that case, the whole cube would be filled up like a box. Valid correlation coefficients, however, exhibit the following relationship:

Figure 18. Valid Region for 3 × 3 Correlation Matrix

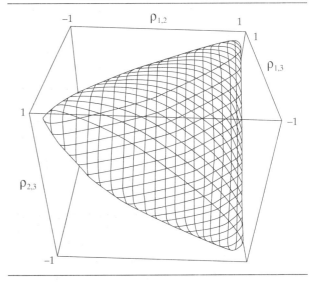

$$\rho_{1,2}^2 + \rho_{1,3}^2 + \rho_{2,3}^2 - 2\rho_{1,2}\rho_{1,3}\rho_{2,3} \le 1.$$

In fact, valid correlation coefficients for a 3×3 correlation matrix can only be the ones inside the tetrahedron-like object. The area inside the cube but outside the tetrahedron is not PSD. A 3×3 correlation matrix with all the correlations equal to 1 would be represented by all angles pointing in the same direction. Although it is possible to put any number of arrows pointing in the same direction on a piece of paper, a correlation matrix of –1, –1, –1 is simply not available because it is not a valid matrix. A 3×3 correlation matrix with the correlations equal to –0.5, –0.5, –0.5 would be a valid matrix, although just at the border of being valid. This matrix would look like a flattened tetrahedron; one corner would be completely flat, and the other angle would be 120 degrees on that corner.

The validity of the correlations an analyst is working with is not immediately obvious from looking at each individual number because the correlation matrix is not simply a bunch of individual numbers. Rather, the matrix is a combined, unified object that has various relationships, some of which can be changed and others of which cannot. Analysts need to understand where the relationships can and cannot be changed. In the case of the 3×3 correlation matrix, if uniform random numbers between –1 and +1 are selected to fill the matrix, then an approximate two-thirds chance of having a valid matrix will exist (because approximately two-thirds of the cube's volume is occupied). For a 4×4 matrix, only a 20 percent chance of having a valid matrix exists if uniform numbers are randomly selected. Only a 4 percent chance of having a valid matrix exists for a 5×5 matrix. If a 20×20 matrix is populated with uniform random numbers between –1 and +1, the probability that a valid matrix exists is less than the chance of winning the lottery. Such a low probability makes sense because several hundred angles exist in 20 dimensions; if one angle is moved, something else, somewhere, has to change.

Another aspect that analysts need to keep in mind is that correlations from different matrixes cannot be mixed. There is no chance that a large, historical correlation matrix will be valid if even one correlation is changed. The reason is that a correlation matrix is not simply a collection of numbers; it is a unified object. Different correlations can be combined in a consistent way to produce a new, valid correlation matrix, but the change has to be coordinated.

Relatively easy-to-use routines can turn covariance matrixes into tables of coordinates. Eigenvalue decomposition (also known as *spectral* analysis or *principal component* analysis) is an example of one of these routines. It is also the routine used to do factor analysis. Correlation and covariance matrixes are

turned into coordinates as follows:

$$\lambda_1, \lambda_2, \lambda_3 = \text{Eigenvalues}\left(\begin{bmatrix} 1 & \rho_{1,2} & \rho_{1,3} \\ \rho_{1,2} & 1 & \rho_{2,3} \\ \rho_{1,3} & \rho_{2,3} & 1 \end{bmatrix}\right)$$

$$\begin{bmatrix} x_1 \\ x_2 \\ x_3 \end{bmatrix} = \begin{matrix} \text{Eigenvectors} \\ \text{(normalized)} \end{matrix}\left(\begin{bmatrix} 1 & \rho_{1,2} & \rho_{1,3} \\ \rho_{1,2} & 1 & \rho_{2,3} \\ \rho_{1,3} & \rho_{2,3} & 1 \end{bmatrix}\right)$$

If B is defined as

$$B = \begin{bmatrix} \sqrt{\lambda_1}x_1 \\ \sqrt{\lambda_2}x_2 \\ \sqrt{\lambda_3}x_3 \end{bmatrix},$$

then

$$B^T B = \begin{bmatrix} 1 & \rho_{1,2} & \rho_{1,3} \\ \rho_{1,2} & 1 & \rho_{2,3} \\ \rho_{1,3} & \rho_{2,3} & 1 \end{bmatrix}$$

Each B can be thought of as a table of coordinates. Once the data are in the form of coordinates, an analyst can stress-test the whole by changing pieces and putting them back together again into a valid covariance matrix. This aspect is important because these models need to be stress-tested as well as used. In stress testing a correlation matrix, one cannot set all the correlations equal to +1 and then set all equal to –1 because, although the first matrix is valid, the second matrix is absolute nonsense. To stress-test a correlation matrix, analysts need to understand that it must be put into the appropriate form.

Summary

Models enable analysts to understand and deal with a certain amount of uncertainty. This presentation illustrated some of the theory and background for inputs into option-pricing models. Such models move practitioners beyond what was done in the 1970s. Although the models may appear complicated, using pictures and geometry helps analysts understand the relationships among parameters in a model, visualize how to use them, see where some of the flaws may lie, and think about how to avoid those flaws.

Derivatives are affected by many parameters, of which volatility is generally the least certain. Using geometry, one can see that correlations and volatilities are interdependent: They are intimately connected. Depending on the number of assets, volatility can be depicted as the distance between points in a triangle or in a tetrahedron, and correlation can be depicted as the angles. With currencies in the picture, geometric figures allow one to see how correlations depend on the currency perspective.

Question and Answer Session

John Zerolis

Question: Must the volatility and correlation relationships hold to prevent arbitrage?

Zerolis: If historical data are used, the covariance matrix will always be valid. The trouble comes if you try to look at implied markets. There is no reason volatility and correlation relationships must hold in the implied cross-volatility markets. If the foreign exchange options are implied, how do you know that the crosses actually have to connect? The market could set prices so that the matrix would not be a triangle. The answer is that if the markets trade options that way, you can construct an option hedge by buying the two little pieces that do not come together and selling the middle part in such a way that you will always make money. At worst, you will always break even; otherwise, you will always make money. There is an arbitrage that will keep that relationship in line. If the matrix is not valid, someone somewhere is giving away money.

Question: Depending on the level of the correlation, does rounding have different implica-

tions in building a covariance matrix or correlation matrix. For example, are the distances on the correlation protractor between 1.00 and 0.95 and between 0.0 and 0.5 equally important in terms of setting the correlation?

Zerolis: One advantage of thinking and understanding correlation as an angle is that it provides an intuitive feel for how the numbers will work. For instance, given those correlations in simple data—a correlation of 0.95 versus a correlation of 1.00 and a correlation of 0.0 versus a correlation of 0.05—the numbers are almost equally far apart. So, you might be tempted to round the 0.95 to 1.00, but this move would be wrong. Taking the correlation from the angular perspective, you can see the much wider difference between 0.95 and 1.00 than between 0.05 and 0.0. Even a higher correlation, 0.99, for example, is still pretty far away from 1.00. Although things may be highly correlated, they may not be substitutes for each other because a significant difference still exists between them.

Question: In Figure 9, if the

German mark is changed to an equity portfolio and the U.S. equities market is left alone, can the same framework be used for performance analysis?

Zerolis: Yes. The geometric picture illustrates risk as a distance, and tracking error is also a distance. To measure a portfolio's performance in relation to a benchmark, you need to determine the distance from the benchmark. For example, if the benchmark is the U.K. equity market, you could determine the distance between your portfolio and that benchmark and determine how much excess return the portfolio provided. You could use an equity basket or an index in the same way. Measuring performance has to do with looking at risk and looking at return, and this approach measures risk as a distance regardless of what benchmark is used as your *numeraire*.

The nice thing about this approach is that it shows you the relationships from the point of view of all the currencies involved. It doesn't pick any one currency and show only that point of view.

Applying Value-at-Risk Measures to Derivatives

David C. Shimko
Vice President, Risk Management Advisory
Bankers Trust Company, New York

Although measuring value at risk has its challenges, VAR is a useful risk-management tool from a portfolio management perspective. VAR can express each component of risk in a security and, combined with measures of expected return, indicate how portfolio managers can increase risk-adjusted returns based on their views. VAR, as a clear indicator of value per unit of risk, will be more and more a part of performance measurement in the future and will ultimately affect portfolio managers' compensation.

Constituents, investors, and staff are pressuring managers to look closely at risk management, especially when derivatives are involved. This presentation focuses on risk management at the strategic level. The purpose is to discuss the main conceptual problems in risk management, raise some difficult questions, and point out the implications of risk management for portfolios with derivatives.

The ideas presented in this presentation come originally from years of experience in applying risk management in the corporate world; the approach is to examine how those techniques can and should be applied by portfolio managers. Value at risk is usually computed for static portfolios, but fund managers are not in the business of holding static portfolios. They are in the business of managing portfolios and earning fees. The approach they need is to think about VAR from the point of view of a business.

The presentation will first present a business-oriented view of the objectives of portfolio management and consider VAR in a portfolio context—what it really means and how useful it is. The discussion will point out the challenges in measuring VAR; without dwelling on the technical side, the discussion will include some of the issues related to "difficult" products, such as path-dependent instruments. The discussion will then turn to how portfolio managers can use VAR and other risk-measurement techniques to be better managers. Finally, I will make some predictions about the use of VAR in the future.

Portfolio Management Objectives

Thinking of the portfolio or fund as a little corporation provides an interesting perspective on risk management. A manager may be continuously taking large or small risks to outperform a benchmark, or at the end of August, if the fund has performed well throughout the year, the manager may be trying to preserve performance relative to the benchmark. Either way, risk management is critical. The manager must consider the likelihood of underperformance throughout the year or take safe positions when the portfolio outperforms. Certainly, no manager will execute strategies that have a high probability of putting the portfolio below the benchmark, because underperformance of the fund brings a drop in the manager's future income. The manager must consider the business impact of outperforming and underperforming—which explains why risk management is so important.

Risk management is critical because the manager needs to know the riskiness of the current portfolio if held statically and also the risk to the business of changes in the portfolio. For example, over the course of a year, based on the current portfolio, what is the likelihood of underperformance if the portfolio deviates from the benchmark by having 10 percent more in gold stocks than the benchmark index? When the portfolio is outperforming the benchmark, is it getting too close to the benchmark return? Are the strategies, including derivatives strategies, the right strategies to minimize the risk of subsequently underperforming, or is the manager simply putting off trading and becoming a closet benchmarker?

The risk in the portfolio management business comes from four sources. First is inherent market risk, on which a lot of the initial work of portfolio management will focus. Identifying the market risk of a portfolio is complex because the instruments—stocks, bonds, foreign exchange, exotic options—can be complex. A number of sources offer help, however, with measuring these risks and their correlations. For example, spreadsheets are available that allow VAR analysis based on variance–covariance matrixes or on linear risk.

A bigger risk in the portfolio management business lies, not in the investment itself, but in the quality of the ideas that lead to the investment. For example, fund managers try to use their views to have better allocations than the benchmark allocation. The big risk is whether the manager's ideas, over time, will regularly be of sufficient quality that the portfolio will consistently outperform the benchmark. This approach applies VAR in a dynamic context; that is, knowing the standard deviations and the correlations among the securities, managers can use the historical performance of their own portfolios to assess their ability to select assets with higher expected returns and lower risks relative to their benchmark. They can use their historical performance to determine the component risks associated with certain strategies or viewpoints. Does a certain view reduce overall portfolio risk over time through dynamic management or does it increase risk? This type of analysis will reveal whether the strategy or view adds enough return to justify the increase in risk or whether the portfolio earns enough return relative to a decrease in risk. That question is difficult for portfolio managers to ask themselves because it touches the core of their value in the business—their ability to consistently capitalize on the value of good investment ideas over time.

Fluctuations in funds flow constitute the resulting risk with which portfolio managers must deal. Some of the fund manager's income is fixed, and some is performance based, but it is all proportional to assets under management. When portfolio management is viewed as a business, underperformance is not merely underperformance; there is a relationship between the fund's performance, investors' actions, and the fund manager's income. VAR, in this view, is not how much the manager underperforms. VAR can translate portfolio performance into actions that the fund investors might take. For example, if the portfolio experiences a 10 percent decline in value and its competitors' performance remains flat, what fraction of the fund will the manager lose? A 10 percent decline in portfolio value could lead to a 30 percent fall in future income if 30 percent of the fund's investors disappear.

The fourth objective of portfolio management is to take risks that are appropriate to the returns to be gained. Taking big risks but achieving only marginal increases in returns does not make sense because those risks could jeopardize the business. A better strategy might be to take only small risks. For example, a fund manager might rank potential investments and determine the return per unit of risk for each investment. Idea #1, Idea #2, and Idea #3 would be ranked according to the quality of each (the expected return). Each idea has an expected return and risk. The risk is the market risk of each investment plus the informational risk—in other words, the value of the manager's opinion. Clearly, the manager wants to diversify among #1, #2, and #3, but the manager also wants to have enough investment in #1 (the best idea) to capitalize on it and have it contribute the most to the portfolio's return. So, the asset allocation process combines analysis of the risk of the underlying instruments with analysis of the risk of the quality of information to figure out if the manager will earn an appropriate return for the risk being taken. In the end, the objective of portfolio management is not simply to beat the benchmark. It is to beat the benchmark on a risk-adjusted basis.

Knowing Risks and Loss Probabilities

Whether based on historical results or prospective analysis, a portfolio manager's view of the probability distribution of returns will be quite different from the market's view for a static portfolio for some time in the future—one month hence, one quarter hence, or one year hence. The market is naive and objective, like an econometrician that has blinders on and sees only the data, not the wider picture. Fund managers have a biased viewpoint. They think they have selected good securities because they do not wear blinders and are not constrained by historical relationships. A fund manager may confidently think a portfolio is excellent and will, like the graph of the manager's view in **Figure 1**, outperform a randomly chosen benchmark by, for example, 2.5 percent in the next year—and with less risk. As Figure 1 shows, the market will have a wider distribution of returns than the fund manager. Fund managers shoot for outperformance and believe in the quality of their views, so they think they have less risk. If you ask fund managers what the VAR of a portfolio is, their answers,

Figure 1. Views of Portfolio Outperformance

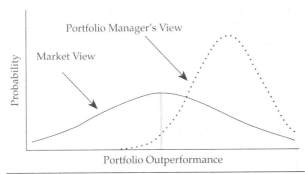

Note: Outperformance defined as portfolio return minus benchmark return for a predetermined time interval.

based on their probability distributions, will tend to be that VAR is low. But an econometrician, ignoring any fundamental considerations and simply looking at the statistics, will say there is a 50 percent chance that this portfolio will underperform and a 5 percent chance that it will underperform by 4 percent or more.

The econometrician will warn the portfolio manager about the extent of the portfolio's risk and indicate how much value the portfolio could lose over a certain period. The portfolio manager's first reaction will be to dismiss that view: "You do not know risk. All you know is Greek letters." But the fund manager has to beat a measure of performance that will be determined by the market, and that measure will be a blind performance measure. It will be based on historical, objective data. So, the fund manager eventually has to look at both sides of the equation, not only how much return the portfolio will achieve but also how much risk the portfolio is assuming.

Investors should not simply accept a fund manager's view of risk; the manager's view of risk is always smaller than the market's. The return a manager earns per unit of risk must exceed the market's expectations. The numerator in the equation is the profit and loss, or the return over benchmark. The denominator is the risk as determined by the market—the guy in the back office wearing the blinders. So, risk management eventually boils down to the denominator of that equation—how much capital the manager puts at risk.

Consider this analogy: Suppose a gas producer spends $100 million developing a gas field. The producer could drill the holes and find nothing there. In that case, the company can sell back the land for some other use for, say, $40 million. So, even though it paid $100 million for the property, the company does not have $100 million at risk. This company's returns should be measured relative only to the $60 million of capital actually at risk. If you buy XYZ stock at

about $110 a share but can sell it for $100 a share, only $10 a share is at risk.

In the fund management business today, returns are generally measured on the basis of the total investment rather than the portion of the investment that is at risk, but this approach will change as investors become smarter. Investors will not ask about the standard deviation, the Sharpe ratio, or other measures that they do not understand. They will want a measure of capital like VAR. A manager who has $5 million in funds and only $1 million of those funds at risk should measure returns as though the $4 million is risk free and the $1 million is managed like a hedge fund. VAR is how much capital a manager actually invests.

VAR in a Portfolio Context

VAR is one measure of risk based on a probability distribution. The VAR is how much a portfolio can lose relative to what it is expected to make. It is the 5 percent, or tail, of that distribution and how much the portfolio can lose up to that point.

The concept of VAR is simple—and intuitive. "How much can we lose" is a natural way of understanding how much is at risk. Implementing VAR is not simple because of the variety of risks that affect the distribution of returns—unexpected funds flows, counterparty credit risk, operational risk, and reputational risk. In addition to affecting future income, unexpected funds flows may affect the returns on the current strategy because the manager may have to suboptimize the current strategy. Counterparty credit risk can have a big influence on return distributions. When a manager does a structured derivative product with a fly-by-night bank, the manager must consider risk from a credit perspective. That nickel squared option may be a great idea designed to make lots of money, but if the bank does not pay, it is of no use to the manager. Most fund managers do not systematically look at credit risk as a part of their risk-taking activity. They do not estimate the likelihood that the counterparty will default and not make good on a major obligation. The nice thing about VAR is that it does allow consideration of credit risk, as well as market risk. Hopefully, managers are not taking operational risk, such as the risk of employing a rogue trader or mismanaging derivatives. Reputational risk is the risk that investors will come to believe that the fund indiscriminately buys every derivative without regard for risk.

Although the concept of VAR is straightforward, not controversial, arguments about the *computation* of VAR abound. Is the worst-case outcome a 5 percent or 1 percent chance of loss? Everyone has a pet technique, and many firms sell proprietary software and services. J.P. Morgan's RiskMetrics is one method. The RAROC (risk-adjusted return on capital) System advanced by Bankers Trust in 1991 is another method.

Someone may say VAR is no good, but it is not clear whether that person is talking about VAR generated from historical simulation or VAR generated from variance–covariance analysis. That probability distribution can be estimated in lots of ways. A major problem is that VAR is usually calculated on a static basis, which is fine for fund managers who do not change their portfolios over time, but few such managers exist.

Better measures of VAR might exist. For example, instead of applying VAR to the portfolio, one could apply it to the franchise value of a fund, which is the business value of a fund or the present value of fee income and incentive income. Franchise value at risk in terms of the present value of future income might be beyond the manager's control because underperformance leads to capital attrition, decreased fee income, and lower franchise value. Fund managers take risk relative to the benchmark, but they may be taking benchmark risk after all, in the sense that performance of the benchmark will affect the present value of fee income. So, a fund manager may have an explicit benchmark and seek protection against fluctuations of the portfolio against the benchmark because the franchise value will be reduced if the portfolio significantly declines in value relative to the benchmark. The manager's decisions may become more business decisions than fund decisions, but I do not currently know how to separate those decisions within the portfolio management process.

Challenges in Measuring VAR

Portfolio managers face challenges in measuring VAR along two dimensions—the approach and the instruments.

RiskMetrics Computation. To understand how controversial the VAR computation can be, consider the RiskMetrics calculation of VAR. The idea of RiskMetrics is to compute the historical variance of a benchmark price series. For a U.S. equity manager, that benchmark series is likely to be the S&P 500 Index. In RiskMetrics, the manager assumes the expected return every day is zero and calculates the squared price change around each day. The novelty of the RiskMetrics technique is that it also uses a rolling volatility estimator, in which greater weight is placed on more-recent observations so that the weighting of the past declines. A decay factor defines how much past volatility information is used to fore-

cast future volatility. Then, the manager calculates correlations similarly, with declining exponential weights. The most recent observations get the greatest weight, and the most distant past observations get the lowest weight.

In calculating variance, the analyst assumes that the mean is zero and constant. In calculating correlations, the analyst assumes that the mean and variance are constant. Indeed, the assumption that the covariance and standard deviation are constant is one of the fundamental problems with the formula for correlation (covariance divided by the product of the standard deviations of two assets). That assumption might work in some markets, but in others, it is wildly wrong. For example, a manager looking at peso returns for the 1992–97 period would probably not be comfortable assuming that the volatility of the peso and the correlations of the peso with other currencies are constant or that a linear relationship exists between the correlations. The very term "variance–covariance correlation" implies a boatload of assumptions.

The first step in RiskMetrics is to measure portfolio risk by converting the portfolio to linear equivalents. An option is converted to its delta equivalent; a bond is converted to its duration equivalent. Then, the analyst measures the risk of a portfolio based on those linear equivalents, assigns that risk to the actual portfolio, and breaks out the risk by the appropriate instrument and by the appropriate exposure.

Historical Variance–Covariance Framework. Variance depends on long-term phenomena that may not be captured in historical simulations. It may not be captured in a RiskMetrics-style calculation, which dampens the impact of volatility over long periods of time. For example, many commodities experience a seasonal variation in volatility. Natural gas is particularly affected; in the winter, natural gas holdings are highly volatile. So, if an analyst uses a historical estimate of correlation that assigns less weight to the last winter than the last summer, the analyst will get completely inappropriate estimates of risk.

Variance may also depend on macroeconomic factors or factors captured in the implied volatility of traded options. An analyst who is trying to estimate the future volatility of German mark positions might look at implied volatility; the more common approach is to look to historical volatility. Both volatility data have benefits and drawbacks. Using historical volatility is not forward looking, but implied volatility may have biases that reflect the relative supply and demand for options in a particular market.

Covariance, or correlation, is messy to analyze, even with a correlation matrix. Measuring the correlation between two variables means assuming a linear relationship between the two variables. Covariance in the global securities markets, however, may depend greatly on price levels. For example, if interest rates soar in one country, correlations between that country's debt securities and those of other countries are bound to change.

The size of price movements can also influence correlations. Two emerging market currencies that are uncorrelated on a daily basis may move together during a liquidity crisis. If an average correlation of, say, 30 percent is assumed, it will be wrong both on a day-to-day basis and in a catastrophic scenario. High correlations for large market moves and low correlations for small moves do not fit into the variance–covariance framework, which assumes a constant correlation.

Correlations between securities depend on the reasons for the market movements. Are the movements caused by flows of capital in the economy or by relative changes in fundamental asset values? For example, U.S. equity correlations increase when the S&P 500 moves a lot.

Finally, certain events may have an impact on correlations that will not be captured in historical data. The implementation of the European Monetary Union is likely to change correlations between the European currencies from their historical patterns.

In summary, before assembling the correlation matrix, the analyst has made four questionable assumptions: that the relationships are linear, that the mean is constant, that the variance is constant, and that the relationship is stable.

Nonlinear Investment Instruments. Most securities, whether a manager realizes it or not, have nonlinear or asymmetrical returns. Bonds are nonlinear functions of interest rates. Structured products may have deliberate nonlinear risks. Convertible bonds or callable bonds have embedded options, and option prices are nonlinear functions of underlying security values. Thus, the embedded options in a bond portfolio will have an impact on the VAR calculation for that portfolio.

The usual remedy used by analysts who try to apply VAR to these complex instruments is a full revaluation. That is, the analyst uses variance–covariance analysis to simulate the underlying instruments, which could be interest rates or security prices. Then, the correct theoretical approach is to revalue all of the options and other securities in the portfolio based on the scenario generated by the underlying values. The analyst revalues the portfolio for each scenario generated and then draws that probability distribution, which could be very different from normal. The worst-case outcome is then the 5 percentile value.

Full revaluation is difficult. It requires pricing models for all the securities the portfolio trades. Models may exist for a lot of instruments, but the analyst needs a pricing model that is as good as a bank's to know what the true risks are. Simulating is time-consuming, and revaluation is even more time-consuming. So, managers look for efficient ways to do them. But although daily revaluation may be fine for reporting purposes, in a fast-moving market, the manager may need intraday revaluations.

Benefits of Using VAR

The major benefit of VAR is that it reveals where the risks are. For example, for a German corporate convertible bond, VAR will indicate each component of risk—currency risk for the non-German investor, corporate credit risk, German mark interest rate risk, and so on. A portfolio may have a large number of instruments but a smaller number of risk factors. Thus, VAR can express the risks of thousands of instruments in terms of 10 or 20 fundamental risks. Aggregating the different sources of risks is beneficial because it may reveal risks that could have been overlooked when they were attached to individual instruments. Then, the manager can manage or optimize such risks. For example, if the aggregation reveals exposure to German interest rates and the manager does not have a view about German interest rates, the manager can consider whether or not that exposure in the portfolio is appropriate.

In theory, portfolio managers use derivatives to take positions that correspond to their views, but a lot of managers unknowingly take positions that add extra risk. For example, if a fund manager thinks gold prices will be above $400, the manager's strategy will typically be to go long gold. The manager may be taking additional risk, however, by taking a long position in gold. A better instrument (a better use of capital) might be a security that pays off only if gold goes above $400. Instead of putting 500 basis points of the fund's value at risk to downturns of the price of gold, the manager puts 50 basis points at risk by buying some binary instrument that pays off only if the price of gold goes above $400. Derivatives allow a manager to leverage the manager's view and get the maximum bang (expected return) for the buck (unit of risk).

One reason portfolio managers have not been interested in VAR is that it focuses on risk, not on return, but a good VAR measure will also tell the manager something about returns. In the example of the German convertible bond, for instance, a good VAR measure, by taking into account all the different sources of risk the convertible has, will identify the source of risk that provides the greatest return. Similarly, when an investor buys oil stocks, a good VAR measure will reveal whether the expected return is based on changes in oil prices or on good management from the oil company. The RAROC System adds this dimension to VAR.

RAROC, as risk-adjusted return on capital, is profitability divided by VAR, so it adds the return dimension to VAR analysis. RAROC indicates return relative to the risk taken. The RAROC formula can be related to the popular Sharpe ratio with the following equation:

$$\text{RAROC} = \text{Sharpe ratio} \times \frac{\sqrt{t}}{z},$$

where t is the VAR evaluation period in years and z is the number of standard deviations in the VAR calculation.

RAROC is similar to the Sharpe ratio—excess return per unit of risk—but it can be applied more broadly. For example, for a plain-vanilla swap, the rate of return is the profit and loss divided by the investment. The cash investment in the swap is zero, which makes the computation of a Sharpe ratio impossible. The economic investment in a swap, however, is the VAR, and the return on investment is the P&L divided by the VAR on the RAROC calculation.

Sculpting Derivative Strategies

RAROC and VAR can be used prospectively to sculpt derivative strategies that fit the portfolio manager's viewpoint. For example, given the probability distributions of the market view and the portfolio manager's view in Figure 1, the manager thinks a particular instrument will increase in value and the risk will be lower than the market expects. Assuming no transaction cost differences between forward contracts, going long, going short, options, and so on, what should the manager do? Rather than simply take a long position in the underlying security, the ideal strategy to follow is one that concentrates probability in the range where the fund manager thinks the probability of payoff will be the greatest. The manager can determine the payoff diagram for a derivative from the following equation:

$$\text{Payoff} = \frac{\text{prob}\,(MGR) - \text{prob}\,(MKT)}{\text{prob}\,(MKT)},$$

This equation requires a simple calculation of percentage difference.

For the manager with the view illustrated in Figure 1, the best strategy is not to buy the instrument but to execute a butterfly strategy with the payoff shown in **Figure 2**. If the manager went long the instrument, the payoff diagram would be a 45 degree line. The butterfly position will pay off when the instrument is in a particular range. In Figure 1, the

portfolio manager's view places a higher probability than the market on one range. So, the idea is to buy probability in that range at market prices. Below the breakeven point (shaded line), the solid line represents the cost of that probability. Above the breakeven point, the dotted line reflects the value of that probability.

Figure 2. Sculpted Strategy: Payoff of a Butterfly Strategy

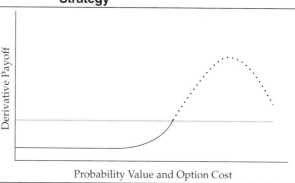

When a manager sculpts derivative strategies, the manager may find that options are more efficient than long positions. A lot of portfolio managers do not like to buy options; they do not like to pay time value. Portfolio management is betting on a view, however, and options allow a manager to make the bet while reducing the consumption of risk capital. Options allow a manager to reduce VAR and thereby increase expected return per unit of VAR. If risk capital is scarce, options are a way to take a large position for the same VAR. So, the stronger the manager's view, the more useful the option. Of course, the manager has to balance that strategy against the transaction costs of using options. The transaction cost is not the full premium, because on average, the buyer gets part of that back by buying options. The real cost is the bid–offer spread in the options, which is higher than for forward positions or underlying long positions.

In some cases, option spreads are more efficient than options. Option spreads are generally used when the portfolio manager places greater probability than the market on either increases or decreases in value. In some cases, the butterfly position like that shown in Figure 2 is the most efficient tool to accomplish a strategy. Butterflies are nothing more than spreads of spreads. With a butterfly position, the manager is betting on a general increase in the market as opposed to taking the full exposure of the upside and the downside. If a manager is long a bull spread, then the manager is short a bull spread at a higher strike.

Designing a derivative strategy with this kind of precision may be difficult, but a manager can also take a current portfolio and work backwards to determine the implied view. An interesting exercise is to determine what view is implied by the strategy taken and instruments used for each portfolio. Then, a manager can analyze whether the chosen strategy or instruments are consistent with the view.

One can infer probability beliefs from strategies. For example, long and short positions in an underlying security indicate that the position taker agrees with the market's assessment of volatility but disagrees with the mean. Long (short) option positions indicate that the position taker believes the mean will be different from market expectations and volatility will be higher (lower). Binary positions indicate that the position taker assigns a higher probability than the market to a binary event. Knockout options indicate that the position taker assigns a low probability that the option will be knocked out.

New Waves in Performance Measurement

Portfolio managers and traders should challenge VAR—not with the idea of destroying it but with the idea of making it better—because VAR will ultimately affect their compensation. On Wall Street, a number of firms are starting to judge their traders based on risk-adjusted contribution, not simply contribution. Bankers Trust has done so since 1991. Salomon Brothers and Lehman Brothers have announced that in some of their areas, the traders are now rewarded on the basis of risk-adjusted contribution, which is profit and loss minus risk charges. As a trader uses up some of the firm's risk capital or consumes some of the firm's ability to bear risk, the trader is charged the required return on risk capital times the VAR. The idea is that a trader must outperform after appropriate charges for risk capital—a clear calculation of value added. It might be thought of as risk-adjusted economic value added. For example, if one trader makes $10 million in a year on $100 million at risk but other portfolio managers are getting a 20 percent return on their risk capital, the one trader is taking on $20 million in risk charges against

$10 million in profits. That trader took on so much risk that it was not worth it for the firm.

In the new wave of performance management, fund managers may be pressured to submit their positions to independent third-party VAR calculation agents. Managers may not be constantly reviewing their portfolios with their investors, but they may be reviewing them with computational agents that calculate VAR and report the portfolios' performance back to the investors. Investors will have an ongoing view of the VAR in their portfolios even if they do not know the exact underlying composition. In this new wave, fund managers must be especially aware of possible abuses of VAR.

Conclusions

Derivatives are only one part of the risk-management picture. Derivatives are extremely useful to those who know how to use them, but no one should even think about using them without clearly understanding what all the risks are. And to know the risks, managers need a way of measuring VAR or some appropriate calculation of the risk in the instruments.

Risk measurement offers opportunities for risk management and for refining portfolio strategies. The discipline of analyzing which risk sources yield the highest returns can provide real benefits. For example, Bankers Trust made a major decision a few years ago to get out of the business of underwriting high-quality debt. The people who built up books, the people who did a lot of customer business, believed this decision destroyed their franchise. But their franchise was destroying value, because the returns were not high enough to compensate for the risks taken. Now, Bankers Trust concentrates in high-yield-debt underwriting, and for good reason: Returns per unit of risk are higher in this market than they were in the high-quality market. Risk management has a real impact on business and a real impact on the future success of any financial institution.

Eventually, VAR reporting and performance measurement will become *de rigueur*. My advice is to get there early. Be among the first to use it instead of the last because you will enjoy the benefits early.

Question and Answer Session

David C. Shimko

Question: Given that the probability of large market moves underestimates their actual occurrence, should analysis focus more on the magnitudes of the distribution tails?

Shimko: This problem is commonly referred to as the peso problem. I can pick a four-year period in the history of Mexico during which returns on the peso were not very volatile, and no matter what kind of historical analysis I do for that period, I cannot pick up the risk or the magnitude of a major devaluation. Similarly, the 1991 Gulf War will not be reflected in some five-year historical series of oil prices. This problem is a computational issue

of VAR, so scenario analysis is useful to improve risk assessments. Scenario analysis complements VAR analysis by requiring estimates of the likelihood of, for example, a major devaluation even if none has occurred in the sample period or the probability of another Gulf War or similar occurrence in the oil industry.

Question: Are credit risk models valuable?

Shimko: The problem with some credit risk models has to do with migration of credit ratings: What is the risk of a particular credit rating changing? The models look at the probabilities of B's turning into BB's or A's, and so on,

over time. The problem with that approach is that credit ratings are slow to change. Yields change a lot faster than credit ratings. So, if you are managing risk of debt instruments, you want to look at changes in the yield spread, not changes in the credit rating, which may be 30–90 days later.

Studies have shown that when firms' debt is downgraded, on average, the change has no impact whatsoever on bond prices. The market has already incorporated that information into the bond prices. A risk model based on such after-the-fact adjustments is not as useful as one based on immediate adjustments to changes in credit quality.

Addressing Derivatives Risk

Maarten Nederlof[1]
Senior Vice President and Director of Investor Risk Management Strategies
Capital Market Risk Advisors, Inc.

Too often, a firm's risk-management infrastructure does not keep pace with new derivative products, and the result can be humiliating investment losses. Firms must adapt their risk-measurement systems to innovations in the financial markets, recognize that a sound risk-management framework includes quantitative and qualitative aspects, and tailor their risk standards to fit their organization.

At Capital Market Risk Advisors, we maintain a list of all the kinds of risks that have caused difficulties, headaches, or losses to our clients during the existence of our firm. Every time we identify a new risk, something that has not been a problem before, we add it to our "Galaxy of Risks," so the list is an evolving, living document that is only a partial listing at any particular time. As **Exhibit 1** shows, the word "derivatives" does not show up on the list, but derivatives have certain characteristics that frequently *contribute* to the risks that are on the list.

The primary risk most major financial institutions faced in the United States from the mid-1700s to about 1980 was "credit risk." During that time, financial institutions greatly refined the analysis of credit risk by building separate credit departments and so on. Unfortunately, in the past 15 years, the instruments used by investment managers have become more complex. This presentation addresses that complexity—why it is happening, what it has caused, and what some of the industry responses have been. The presentation introduces a framework for managing risk today and points out the help firms can find for their risk-management efforts in the guidelines proposed by the Risk Standards Working Group.

Risk-Management Challenge

To identify problems related to derivatives use, our firm tracks the occasions when people publicly disclose that they have lost some money and that derivatives were involved. So, two things have to happen

for a problem to be identified as related to derivatives: The problem has to be publicly disclosed, and the person has to finger derivatives as a contributor (or the key) to the losses. The losses do not have to be in the derivatives themselves; they can be from any aspect of the strategy in which derivatives were used.

At this point, defining "derivative instrument" will be useful. A preferred approach is to strip away the highly legal and carefully engineered definitions and go with the essence of the instruments, including securities with embedded derivatives. For example, many of the situations that led to highly publicized losses related to "derivatives" were losses from collateralized mortgage obligations (CMOs), structured securities, and similar instruments that were slipped into portfolios because they met the technical guideline of being AAA rated, agency issued, and a physical security. These instruments are technically physical securities under the legal and regulatory framework, but they frequently have embedded "derivative" features. Nothing is wrong with innovating within the guidelines, but managers and clients have to understand the implications for their management, measurement, and oversight responsibilities.

Publicly reported cumulative losses from derivatives were relatively flat until about 1993 or 1994. (Unfortunately, putting a value on the losses is fraught with issues: If an investor lost money on one thing but had a hedge on the other side, can it be called a loss?) In 1994, as **Figure 1** shows, the losses soared up—from about $4 billion to about $14 billion—and they have continued to climb, but at a lower rate. These numbers, however, must be viewed in context. In 1994, all owners of U.S. Treasury debt together lost more than $250 billion, but those losses

---

[1]Mr. Nederlof is now managing director, global equity derivatives, at Deutsche Morgan Grenfell, Inc.

Exhibit 1. Galaxy of Risks

Accounting risk	Hedging risk	Political risk
Bankruptcy risk	Horizon risk	Prepayment risk
Basis risk	Iceberg risk	Publicity risk
Call risk	Interest rate risk	Raw data risk
Capital risk	Interpolation risk	Regulatory risk
Collateral risk	Knowledge risk	Reinvestment risk
Commodity risk	Legal risk	Rollover risk
Concentration risk	Limit risk	Suitability risk
Contract risk	Liquidity risk	Systemic risk
Credit risk	Market risk	Systems risk
Currency risk	Modeling risk	Tax risk
Curve construction risk	Netting risk	Technology risk
Daylight risk	Optional risk	Time-lag risk
Equity risk	Personnel risk	Volatility risk
Extrapolation risk	Phantom risk	Yield-curve risk

Note: Partial listing.

Source: Capital Market Risk Advisors.

Figure 1. Publicly Disclosed Derivatives Losses, as of November 4, 1997

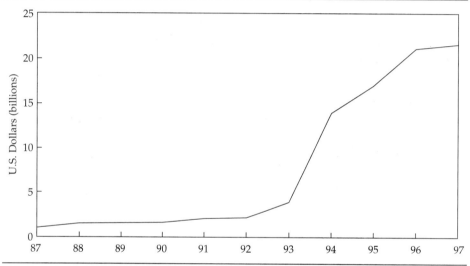

Note: Cumulative losses (pretax equivalents).

Source: Capital Market Risk Advisors.

have not received the press coverage that losses from derivatives have. Also, in the context of the size of the markets, derivatives losses are not nearly as significant in terms of losses per unit of traded assets or traded instruments.

Many people look at the increase in losses since the early 1990s and believe it must be related to interest rates because 1994 was the year that rates moved in an almost unprecedented manner (they moved similarly in the late 1950s, but people do not have very long memories). If interest rates were the sole cause, however, the losses should have leveled off after 1994; in fact, they have definitely continued to increase.

Breaking the losses into categories provides a clearer picture of where investment management

firms experienced losses and helps identify the nature of firm risks. **Figure 2** shows the losses by the investment world—that is, public and private funds and their advisors—as a portion of the total losses as of November 1997 and as a portion of losses on various types of instruments. (The non-investment-world would include other types of financial institutions.) The investment world had its share of losses but took many fewer losses in exchange-traded derivatives. One explanation for this phenomenon is that because exchange-traded instruments are overt derivatives (as opposed to securities with embedded derivatives), the investment world reduces the possibility of loss on exchange-traded instruments by explicitly addressing the risks in its investment process guidelines and procedures.

Figure 2. Public and Private Funds' Share of Derivative Losses, as of November 4, 1997

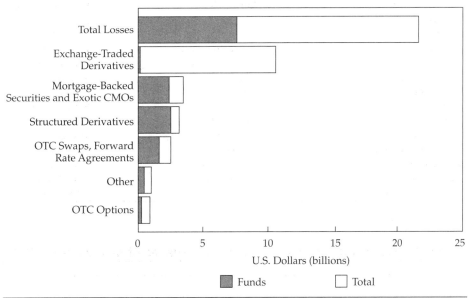

Note: Publicly declared losses on a cumulative basis; pretax equivalents.
Source: Capital Market Risk Advisors.

The increased complexity in risk management is also a function of the growth in the derivatives markets. For example, swap trading and trading in engineered securities, which started at about the same time in the 1980s, have soared—to more than $4 trillion for engineered securities and more than $10 trillion for swaps. So, activity in derivative instruments has exploded.

Pressure to innovate and increase portfolio alpha

forces the investment business to increase the complexity of its activities, which can lead to increased losses. **Figure 3** summarizes how those pressures build up to force a reexamination of the firm's risk management. Competition is a catalyst in this process and moves investment management firms around this cycle until the firm reaches a turning point and must reevaluate its risk-management policies. The investment business is characterized by incredible

Figure 3. Risk-Management Turning Point

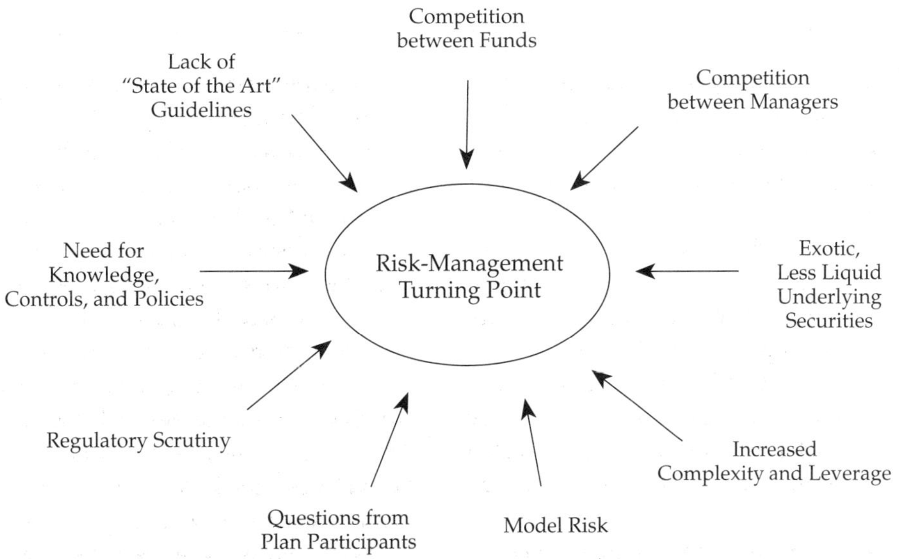

Competition between Funds

Lack of "State of the Art" Guidelines

Competition between Managers

Need for Knowledge, Controls, and Policies

Risk-Management Turning Point

Exotic, Less Liquid Underlying Securities

Regulatory Scrutiny

Increased Complexity and Leverage

Questions from Plan Participants

Model Risk

Source: Capital Market Risk Advisors.

competitiveness—among funds and among managers. Investors look to their investment managers to provide extra returns; after all, alpha is good. To consistently outperform their various benchmarks, however, managers have to constantly innovate— look for new instruments, new opportunities, new markets. The best managers find those innovations, but doing so frequently moves them into more complex and illiquid instruments.

In this way, funds increase in general complexity simply because of the passage of time. Nothing is wrong with this process per se; it can be what clients expect from their investment managers. The problem is that the firm's infrastructure frequently does not keep up with the complexity of the products it uses.

In addition, firms' investment choices may be subject to a fair amount of model risk. More and more firms rely on models to produce valuations and risk estimates for instruments in their portfolios. Whether it is how the yield curve was built to value a corporate bond or how option models estimate the implied volatility of an options portfolio or a single option, firms are sensitive to model risk. Even small changes in assumptions can have a great impact on the final value and risk estimates. Many firms, unfortunately, do not spend much time addressing model risk.

Then, the firm becomes subject to questions from clients about risk; such questioning has increased in the past few years. Questions from plan sponsors and participants lead to increased regulatory scrutiny and pressure.

Finally, the firm realizes that it needs knowledge, control, and policies to manage the complicated risks it has assumed. As part of that realization, a lot of firms are reviewing their existing investment guidelines and finding them no longer as state of the art as they once were. For example, consider these typical but inadequate guidelines:

- Fixed-income investments must be AAA rated and less than two years to maturity. Certainly, managers can find a lot of paper that is AAA and two years to maturity. The question is: Is that restrictive guideline as necessary as it used to be? When many analysts first learned about duration, the rule was that the duration of an instrument could never be longer than its maturity. But that dictum is no longer the case. Most of the investments in the Orange County Investment Pool fell within the duration guideline of two years to maturity and AAA rating. Unfortunately, some of the instruments had *effective* durations of 15 years.[2] A frequent addition to this

guideline is to make sure the bonds are government issued only. But what does "government issued only" mean? What about government agencies, which are frequent issuers of structured notes?

- The risk must be low-interest-rate risk.
- Instruments must have a high degree of liquidity.
- Hedging (with currency forward contracts) is allowed but not speculating. What if a manager buys some Swiss bonds and then decides he or she really does not want to use Swiss forward contracts to hedge that currency exposure but will instead use German mark contracts. Is that hedging or speculation? This type of "proxy hedging," which is the term for this example, is widespread. Whenever I ask a roomful of chief investment officers or other managers whether proxy hedging constitutes hedging or speculating, I get a mix of votes. After the fact, when the board of directors is under pressure or regulatory scrutiny, they will probably not agree with the manager or trader's interpretation.

What do these terms mean? Many of the disputes between money managers and their clients or between fiduciaries and the people whose assets they manage have involved major legal disagreements over the interpretation of these types of ambiguous terms.

Many other issues arise with such guidelines. So, defining these terms, articulating and writing down as many specifics as possible, will help reduce the chances of a misunderstanding.

Innovations in financial instruments often necessitate changes in risk measurement. **Figure 4** illustrates how innovations in risk measurement track the development of the swaps and engineered securities markets, measured in terms of notional trading volume. In the late 1970s, risk controls were initially based solely on credit ratings, single monthly mortality (SMM) rates for mortgage pools, and holding-period yields. Then, as the first currency swaps entered the picture in 1980, the first CMOs in 1983, and the first caps and collars in 1984, more and more risk-measurement models were built. Firms produced risk-management reports, limited exposure based on duration buckets, and continued to limit exposure based on credit considerations. In the late 1980s, firms started looking at option-adjusted spreads and effective duration for measuring exposure to fixed-income securities with embedded options. With the explosion of derivatives activity in the 1990s, firms went from managing the Greeks— including delta and gamma—to managing reserves for liquidity and model risk and measuring value at risk. On the timeline of development and measurement, innovations appear about every six months.

---

[2]For further reading on the Orange County bankruptcy, see Philippe Jorion, "Lessons from the Orange County Bankruptcy," *Journal of Derivatives* (Summer 1997):61–66.

Figure 4. Growth of Derivatives and Evolution of Risk Measures

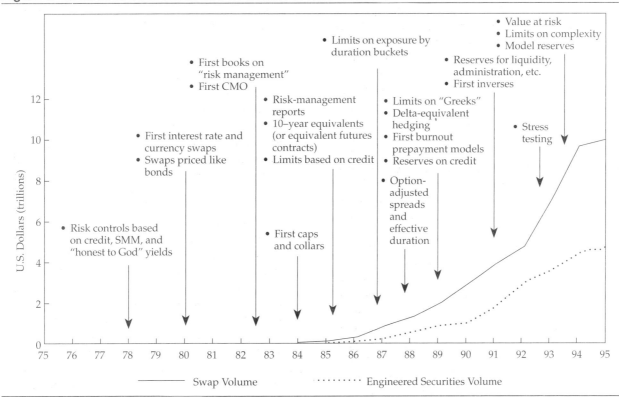

Source: Capital Market Risk Advisors.

Operations and risk oversight managers often find out that they need a new measurement tool when they discover that their old measurement framework does not explain the price behavior of a new instrument or an existing instrument in new market conditions.

Innovations in derivative products are constant, and risk-measurement tools must change as new products are developed. The result of this increasing complexity is that managers can never put a measurement system into place and bank on it forever. They have to constantly revise it, keep up with the literature, and keep up with the new instruments.

Unfortunately, this process can require more spending on measurement systems than a lot of firms are used to. So, not surprisingly, as long as markets were calm or bullish and people were not having adverse experiences with the new instruments, they did not pay a lot of attention to the measurement problem. When losses occurred, the adverse experiences raised the profile of failing risk-measurement systems. The question is: What should managers do about measuring and managing the complex risks introduced by innovations in the business?

Risk-Management Framework

Numerous qualitative as well as quantitative aspects go into the management of risk. **Exhibit 2** lists some aspects that are important to a framework. Only about a third are quantitatively based—that is, are limits or measurements. Many parts of a good system involve nonquantitative aspects—education and knowledge, policies, random audits. The risks that Exhibit 1 did not list are the risks that the manager cannot control—the act of God, a large structural shift in the markets, the legislative change in the treatment for taxes. Such risks are always present, but a firm's insensitivity to them can be reduced by effectively addressing the other factors. Not addressing one or two aspects of this framework, combined with some bad luck, can be enough to give a manager and the manager's client a bad surprise in the future.

Once a manager decides to control risk, the challenge is how to actively manage it. Money management firms and funds have very different attitudes toward risk. Some approaches are extreme, with stringent guidelines that explicitly state, "If it's not written here, you can't do it." To bring a new product to these firms, a manager has to write the clients a letter, appeal to the client's board, and wait while the board discusses it at their next quarterly meeting—by

Exhibit 2. Quantitative and Qualitative Factors in a Risk-Management Framework

Quantitative	Qualitative
Value at risk	Overarching guidelines
Marginal impact of traders/managers	Independent risk oversight
Stress tests	Risk-management guidelines
Risk-adjusted performance measures	Trader/manager guidelines
Limits policies	Risk-measurement guidelines
Dynamic updating	Procedures and controls
Complex security pricing	Random audits
Multidimensional risk monitoring	Education and knowledge
	Timely information reporting
	Checks and balances

Source: Capital Market Risk Advisors.

which time, the opportunity may be long gone. This type of risk management slows innovation and frustrates managers.

At the other end of the spectrum are firms and funds that do no risk management; they hire experts and let them do their thing because, after all, they are the experts. The minimalists operate on trust; they rely on the firm's culture to control risk and do the "right thing." Of course, this approach often leaves room for adverse innovation. The major problem is that all of these firms have fiduciary obligations. How does the firm know the so-called experts are experts? Just because everyone else hires them and calls them experts, does relying on that consensus meet one's fiduciary obligation to determine whether they are, indeed, experts?

The investment management firm has to decide where to position itself on this spectrum. The firm must decide how stringent it wants to be and how much risk management it wants to carry out itself. An investment management firm that decides to control everything itself will need significant infrastructure for monitoring the firm's activities. A firm that decides to use the minimalist approach will have to perform greater up-front due diligence to make sure it can rely on the people that manage the firm's risk.

Risk Standards

Because many investment professionals are faced with the challenge of monitoring risk, this section discusses where they can turn to for help. All of the advisory documents put out by government entities and industry groups around the world that deal with risk issues or issues pertaining to interactions with clients—large studies, such as those of the Group of Thirty, and the codes of conduct or principles and practices distributed by various regulators—have six minimum criteria in common. Although regulators in the United States do not have comprehensive, explicit rules about risk management, whether

involving derivatives or otherwise, most U.S. investments are managed pursuant to a prudent person standard, which requires reasonable care. If such explicit rules ever evolve in the United States, however, chances are that they will contain these same six elements. So, the six elements can be viewed as the writing on the wall:

- Some kind of *risk measurement*.

- An independent *risk-oversight* function. This criterion is controversial for the money management business. What does such oversight mean, and how would it work in a small money management firm? If the firm is only three people, who monitors whom and when?

- Requisite *knowledge and systems*. The standard setters believe the firm should know what it is doing. The U.S. Department of Labor (DOL) has filed its first suit under ERISA against a fund that invested in CMOs and clearly did not understand what it was doing, nor did it seek the appropriate expertise.[3] The fund lost $3 million out of $100 million. The DOL suit alleges that the fund's trustees did not perform the necessary due diligence nor heed the advice of its other expert advisors. On March 28, 1996, the DOL wrote a letter to the Office of the Comptroller of the Currency driving home the point that derivatives are no different from any other kind of instrument and that if a firm does not have the expertise to handle derivatives in-house, the firm must get external assistance.

- Specific *written policies and controls*. Money management firms, believing that all their managers know what they are supposed to do, do not like to write policy manuals. One of the first things that will happen in any kind of investigation, however, is that the regulators or lawyers will

---

[3]*Reich v. Trustees of the Connecticut Plumbers and Pipefitters Pension Fund.*

ask for all the firm's policy manuals. If the firm does not have policy manuals, it will have a difficult time arguing that it had the appropriate risk-management policies. The second question will be, "Who here has read this policy manual?" They will depose everybody and ask them individually, "Have you read the manual? Have you read this page?" Ultimately, the question is *how* people in the organization find out exactly what is the right thing to do. The question is hard to answer unless the firm has actually written it down. Therefore, revision of written policies is one of the first places people start when updating the firm's risk management. They have procedures, but they have not articulated them.

- Daily (or frequent) *marking to market* of positions.
- *Stress testing and simulation.*

Marking to market, stress testing, and simulation are designed to give managers an accurate handle on their investments, the values of those investments, and the risks in those investments.

Issues Specific to Institutional Investors.

Most previous risk advisory documents applied to banks and securities dealers, not money management firms. Indeed, one of the problems the money management industry faces is the lack of guidelines that deal specifically with its problems. For example, the money management industry tends to have long time horizons—holding periods that are significantly longer than those of banks or dealers and evaluation periods that are longer than for trading desks, which are evaluated almost overnight. In addition, money managers deal with a broad array of asset classes.

Institutional investors also deal with multiple outside investment firms and managers. A typical fund structure has 10–15 external money managers. Major broker/dealers tend to bring all the people they need in-house. These firms set their own standards, monitor all of their activities, and fire employees if they do not follow the rules. With 10–15 external money managers sprinkled all over the world, adequate risk control or quality assurance is difficult to maintain.

Funds and money managers also still focus primarily on historical performance, not risk-adjusted performance, whereas the dealer community has started examining performance of their trading businesses on a risk-adjusted basis.

Finally, there is the issue of who is a fiduciary. Dealers and banks avoid fiduciary responsibility, whereas the employees of almost any type of investment management organization clearly have fiduciary responsibilities. The question is: What are those responsibilities?

The Risk Standards Working Group. Many practitioners wanted some list of standards or minimum requirements for money managers but did not know who to turn to for guidelines. In response to all this uncertainty, a group of 11 individuals from a variety of organizations got together in April 1996 to begin work on some standards. The group members looked at numerous other documents but realized they were inadequate for the money management business. They also realized that various industry constituencies—from regulators to pension fund clients—had opinions on risk standards and that if each constituency were to develop its own guidelines, money managers could, for example, receive a different requirement list from each client. All they would do all day long is fill out risk questionnaires, which would significantly affect their ability to manage money. Therefore, the Working Group decided that well-thought-out risk guidelines that were somewhat standardized for the entire industry would be the best approach.

The Working Group's mission was to create a set of risk standards for institutional investment managers and institutional investors—for both money managers and funds. After the first draft was written, the Working Group solicited comments from many people—money management firms, academics, banks, asset owners, plan sponsors, investment managers, legal advisors, industry groups and associations, rating agencies, auditors and accountants, and national and international regulators. The final document, released in November 1996, contains 20 risk standards that focus on three areas—management, measurement, and oversight. **Exhibit 3** summarizes the standards, but I encourage you to read the full document because it provides detailed descriptions of each standard and some examples of their application.[4]

The Working Group's document is not meant to be a simple rule book that applies to all money managers. Implementation must vary by type of institution. A pension cannot simply take this document, put its name on it, and announce that the standards are now its policy document for risk: "Sign it and swear that you will abide by it." The document sets high standards—something to aim for—and is intended to provide a structure for a firm's risk-management policy. Making the standards work for any firm is likely to require time, money, and talented people. No single institution is likely to meet all the standards to the highest degree, but most institutions can narrow down the challenge, assess their practices against the

---

[4]The final copy of these risk standards can be found on the Internet at www.cmra.com, www.gte.com/g/ghinv.html, and several other places.

Exhibit 3. Standards from the Risk Standards Working Group

Management Risk Standards	Measurement Risk Standards	Oversight Risk Standards
Acknowledgment of fiduciary responsibilities	Valuation procedures	Comparison of manager strategies with compensation and investment activity
Approved written policies, definitions, guidelines, and investment documentation	Valuation reconciliation, bid–offer adjustments, and overrides	Independent review of methodologies, models, and systems
Independent risk oversight, checks and balances, written procedures and controls	Risk measurement and risk–return attribution analysis	Review process for new activities
Clearly defined organizational structure and key roles	Risk-adjusted return measures	Due diligence, policy compliance, and guideline monitoring
Consistent application of risk policies	Stress testing	
Adequate education, systems and resources, and backup and disaster recovery plans	Backtesting	
Identification and understanding of key risks	Assessing model risk	
Setting risk limits		
Routine reporting, exception reporting, and escalation procedures		

Source: Capital Market Risk Advisors.

risk standards, and rest assured that their efforts will address the concerns of the broadest number of clients.

Conclusion

Successful investment management firms and institutional investors will continue the trend of increased innovation and complexity in investment activities. The proportion of derivatives and other complex instruments in portfolios will continue to grow, taxing the risk management, measurement, and oversight activities of managers and their clients. The emergence of risk standards indicates that the industry, because of some painful lessons learned in recent years and in response to increased interest in the topic by their clients, is increasing attention to the issue of risk management.

Question and Answer Session

Maarten Nederlof

Question: How well do institutional investors actually meet the recommended standards?

Nederlof: Based on firms' own assessments of how well they meet the standards—from funds that might be called professionally managed to organizations that have half a person running a pension fund that is largely outsourced—they are frequently in the 40–60 percent range. Talking in terms of percentages is always dangerous, of course, because, as I pointed out, the lack of only one of these policies could give you a lot of grief, but it is important to note that firms do deal with the issues to a large degree. From that point, getting to the higher levels of compliance is actually not hard. Frequently, all that is needed is dedicating resources to it.

Not many firms have resources specifically dedicated to compliance with the risk-management standards set forth by the Working Group, perhaps because the document has not yet been widely circulated. Recently, however, pressure to manage risk has increased. The Organization for Economic Cooperation and Development recently sent the standards out to all its member countries—the national regulators and central banks—as an example of how to approach investment risk management. Many emerging market governments have approached the Working Group for a model of where to start in regulating risk. So, interest in the standards as a way of raising the bar in regard to risk management is picking up in the regulatory community.

Firms should be careful about vouching that they carry out various aspects of risk oversight. Several large money management firms have announced publicly that they put together a team, spent a great deal of money, worked very hard for a couple of years, and now think they are largely compliant. Such statements are risky because if the firm hasn't done something to somebody else's satisfaction, the statement may come back to haunt the firm in the future.

Self-Evaluation Examination

1. According to Hill, which of the following statements about options and futures is correct?
   I. An option is rich or cheap depending on its implied volatility relative to the historical volatility of the stock or index.
   II. Futures contracts on the Nasdaq 100 Index have smaller mispricings in nearby futures contracts and the calendar spread than do S&P 500 Index futures.
   III. The dollar trading volume in the underlying stocks is significantly greater than the dollar amount that trades in stock index futures.
   IV. A futures contract produces symmetrical returns and bears the full risk and return of the underlying security or portfolio.
   A. I and III.
   B. II and IV.
   C. I and IV.
   D. III.

2. Hill suggests that the biggest growth in derivatives use in the 1990s has been in which of the following:
   A. Stock index options.
   B. Global asset allocation strategies.
   C. Portfolio insurance.
   D. Credit derivatives.

3. Which of the following, according to Hill, are the primary influence on the level of derivatives activity?
   A. Volatility and market direction.
   B. Macroeconomic events.
   C. Regulatory environments.
   D. All of the above.

4. According to Hill, restrictions on short selling tend to contribute to richness in futures pricing.
   A. True.
   B. False.

5. Hill states that which of the following strategies improves the income yield on stocks that have high volatility and no dividend yield?
   A. Selling puts.
   B. Buying calls.
   C. Selling calls.
   D. Selling zero-premium collars.

6. According to Chance, which of the following derivatives protects floating-rate note issuers from rising interest rates?
   A. Entering into a pay fixed/receive floating interest rate swap.
   B. Buying an interest rate call option.
   C. Buying an interest rate cap.
   D. All of the above.

7. Which of the following statements regarding interest rate swaptions is correct according to Chance?
   I. A receiver swaption decreases in value as interest rates decline.
   II. The buyer of a swaption faces no credit risk; all of the credit risk is embedded in the underlying swap.
   III. The seller of a payer swaption accepts having to enter into a swap at a below-market rate as the fixed-rate receiver.
   IV. The seller of a receiver swaption accepts having to enter into a swap at an above-market rate as the fixed-rate payer.
   A. I and II.
   B. II and III.
   C. III and IV.
   D. I and IV.

8. Which of the following swap structures allows a fixed-income portfolio manager to take advantage of relative changes in the shape of the yield curve between two countries?
   A. Index-amortizing swap.
   B. Differential swap.
   C. Currency swap.
   D. Constant maturity swap.

9. According to Chance, which of the following statements describes credit derivatives?
   I. Credit derivatives will improve loan pricing as financial markets become more integrated.
   II. A highly liquid market exists for credit derivatives.
   III. Standard definitions of credit events determine the payoff of credit derivatives.
   IV. Credit derivatives allow investors to separate market risk from credit risk.

©Association for Investment Management and Research

A. II and III.
B. I and IV.
C. I and II.
D. II and IV.

10. According to Ho, the main difference between a generic currency swap and a plain-vanilla pay-fixed swap is that the currency swap involves an exchange of principal on the swap termination date.
    A. True.
    B. False.

11. According to Ho, which of the following derivative structures makes the notional principal amount a less meaningful measure of risk exposure?
    A. Quanto structured notes.
    B. Power swaps.
    C. Rainbow options.
    D. Index-amortizing swaps.

12. Which of the following risk measures represents the price sensitivity of a bond or a swap to different points along the yield curve?
    A. Macaulay duration.
    B. Modified duration.
    C. Key-rate duration.
    D. Effective duration.

13. According to Zerolis, which of the following statements correctly describes option-pricing behavior?
    A. A long-dated option is almost always worth more than a short-dated option with the same strike price.
    B. As the time to expiration increases, the value of volatility decreases because there is only a remote chance the option will expire in the money.
    C. When a put option is deep in the money, delta is approximately 50 percent.
    D. Vega measures an option value's sensitivity to changes in interest rates.

14. Using volatility-and-correlation geometry, correlations are the _____ of each _____ of the triangle and volatility is the _____ of each _____ of the triangle.
    A. Length, side, cosecant, angle.
    B. Cosines, angle, length, side.
    C. Perpendicular bisector, side, sine, angle.
    D. Length, side, cosine, angle.

15. According to Zerolis, which of the following geometric figures represents the correlations between four currencies?
    A. Triangle.
    B. Tetrahedron.
    C. Isosceles triangle.
    D. Equilateral triangle.

16. Shimko believes that value at risk (VAR) can be used to accomplish which of the following portfolio management objectives?
    A. Quantify inherent market risk.
    B. Translate portfolio performance into actions that investors in a fund might take.
    C. Evaluate view-driven strategies.
    D. All of the above.

17. According to Shimko, VAR will be increasingly used to evaluate portfolio managers' performance and determine their compensation.
    A. True.
    B. False.

18. Nederlof defines which of the following elements as part of a sound risk-management program?
    A. Traders marking their positions to market on a monthly basis.
    B. Mandatory use of VAR analysis.
    C. Broad policies and controls on derivatives use.
    D. None of the above.

Self-Evaluation Answers

1. **C.** Futures contracts on the Nasdaq 100 have larger mispricings in nearby futures contracts and the calendar spread than do S&P 500 index futures. The larger mispricings occur because the stocks in the Nasdaq 100 have wider bid–offer spreads than stocks in the S&P 500. The dollar trading volume of the underlying stocks is typically only a fraction of the dollar amount that trades in stock index futures.

2. **B.** The biggest growth in derivatives use in the 1990s has been in global asset allocation strategies. Portfolio insurance was popular in the 1980s, but its popularity has waned. The credit derivatives market is just beginning to evolve but may experience significant growth in the future.

3. **D.**

4. **B.** Restrictions on short selling tend to contribute to cheapness in futures pricing because selling futures acts as a substitute for short selling. Investors are willing to sell futures below fair value because they have no other way of creating a short market position.

5. **C.** Selling calls is a way of improving the income yield on stocks that have high volatility and no dividend yield. For example, investors might want to own a low-dividend company but want to transform the holding into something that has a lower profile. Instead of selling the stock, they can sell a call against a portion of the position and translate some of the potential gain into an income yield from the call sale. Selling calls is similar to trading capital gains for an up-front substitute for dividend yield.

6. **D.** Combined with an existing floating-rate note, a pay fixed/receive floating interest rate swap effectively converts a floating-rate liability to a fixed-rate bond and hedges the borrower from rising interest rates. Buying an interest rate call option gives the holder the right to make a fixed-rate payment and receive a floating-rate payment. Buying an interest rate cap is typically a series or combination of interest rate call options that expire on different dates. When the exercise dates coincide with the interest payment dates on an underlying floating rate note, the buyer is effectively insulated from rising interest rates.

7. **C.** A receiver swaption represents the right to enter a swap as a fixed-rate receiver/floating-rate payer and *increases* in value when interest rates decline. The buyer of the swaption accepts the risk of the writer defaulting. That is, the buyer of the option to enter into the swap risks the possibility that when the time comes to exercise it, the party on the other side will have gone bankrupt and not be able to enter into the swap.

8. **B.** See Chance's presentation.

9. **B.** The market for credit derivatives is evolving and not yet very liquid. A lot of transactions occur, but the transactions are based on the credit of a single counterparty, not generic, marketwide credit risk. One of the problems in determining the payoff of credit derivatives is defining a credit event.

10. **A.**

11. **B.** The notional amount of a power swap has little meaning because the investor may be betting three or four times more than the notional principal amount. A power swap effectively increases the interest rate bet by multiplying or compounding the reference index. An investor in a power note or swap wants to obtain extremely high returns from small changes in the reference rate or index over short periods of time.

12. **C.** As Ho explains, key-rate duration, which is an extension of the single-factor duration measures (Macaulay duration and modified duration), represents the price sensitivity of a bond or swap to changes in different points (i.e., key rates) along the relevant yield curve. For example, a two-year swap has two key rates. The effective duration of a swap or bond is simply the sum of all the key-rate durations.

13. A. As the time to expiration for an option increases, the value of volatility increases because more time exists for the underlying security to change price and for the option to move into the money. When a put option is deep in the money, delta is 100 percent. Vega measures an option's sensitivity to changes in volatility; rho measures its sensitivity to changes in interest rates.

14. B. According to Zerolis, the correlations are the cosines of each angle. Volatility is expressed as a distance, the length of each side, using any unit as long as the same unit is used to measure each volatility.

15. B. When correlations between four sets of returns are involved, a three-dimensional figure is needed.

16. D.

17. A.

18. D. Nederlof lists the following six elements of a sound risk-management framework: some kind of risk measurement, independent risk oversight, requisite knowledge and systems, specific written policies and controls, frequent (*daily*) marking to market of positions, and stress testing and simulation.

Selected Publications

AIMR

AIMR Performance Presentation Standards Handbook, 2nd edition, 1997

Asian Equity Investing, 1998

Deregulation of the Electric Utility Industry, 1997

Economic Analysis for Investment Professionals, 1997

Equity Valuation and Research Techniques, 1998

Finding Reality in Reported Earnings, 1997

Global Bond Management, 1997

Implementing Global Equity Strategy: Spotlight on Asia, 1997

Investing in Small-Cap and Microcap Securities, 1997

Investing Worldwide VIII: Developments in Global Portfolio Management, 1997

Managing Currency Risk, 1997

Standards of Practice Casebook, 1996

Standards of Practice Handbook, 7th edition, 1996

Research Foundation

Blockholdings of Investment Professionals
by Sanjai Bhagat, Bernard S. Black, and Margaret M. Blair

Company Performance and Measures of Value Added
by Pamela P. Peterson, CFA, and David R. Peterson

Controlling Misfit Risk in Multiple-Manager Investment Programs
by Jeffery V. Bailey, CFA, and David E. Tierney

Country Risk in Global Financial Management
by Claude B. Erb, CFA, Campbell R. Harvey, and Tadas E. Viskanta

Economic Foundations of Capital Market Returns
by Brian D. Singer, CFA, and Kevin Terhaar, CFA

Initial Dividends and Implications for Investors
by James W. Wansley, CFA, William R. Lane, CFA, and Phillip R. Daves

Interest Rate Modeling and the Risk Premiums in Interest Rate Swaps
Robert Brooks, CFA

Sales-Driven Franchise Value
Martin L. Leibowitz